University of California
San Diego

THE CAMPUS GUIDE

University of California San Diego

AN ARCHITECTURAL TOUR BY

Dirk Sutro

WITH PHOTOGRAPHS BY

David Hewitt

and

Anne Garrison

PRINCETON ARCHITECTURAL PRESS

NEW YORK

Published by
Princeton Architectural Press
37 East Seventh Street
New York, New York 10003

For a free catalog of books, call 1.800.722.6657.
Visit our website at www.papress.com.

Series Editor: Nancy Eklund Later
Editor: Linda Lee
Designer: Bree Anne Apperley
Mapmaker: Matt Knutzen

Special thanks to: Nettie Aljian, Sara Bader, Nicola Bednarek,
Janet Behning, Becca Casbon, Carina Cha, Tom Cho, Penny (Yuen
Pik) Chu, Carolyn Deuschle, Russell Fernandez, Pete Fitzpatrick,
Wendy Fuller, Jan Haux, Laurie Manfra, John Myers, Katharine Myers,
Steve Royal, Dan Simon, Andrew Stepanian, Jennifer Thompson, Paul
Wagner, Joseph Weston, and Deb Wood of Princeton Architectural
Press —Kevin C. Lippert, publisher

Library of Congress Cataloging-in-Publication Data

Sutro, Dirk.
University of California, San Diego : an architectural tour / by Dirk
Sutro ; with photographs by David Hewitt and Anne Garrison.
    p. cm. — (The campus guide)
Includes bibliographical references and index.
ISBN 978-1-56898-860-3 (alk. paper)
1. University of California, San Diego—Buildings—Guidebooks. 2.
Architecture—California—San Diego—Guidebooks. I. Title.
LD781.S2S88 2010
378'.19620979498—dc22
                                                        2009045012

CONTENTS

Readers ranging from architects and planners to University of California, San Diego alumni, faculty, students, and parents, and travelers from around the world will find this book useful. It gives an overview of campus planning and architecture, interwoven with the story of the people, politics, and social changes that shaped the campus.

The book opens with an introduction that covers the history of the university's modern architecture, as well as UCSD's evolution from a laboratory in a boathouse at the Hotel del Coronado (the beginning of what would become Scripps Institution of Oceanography) to the maturation of Scripps during the postwar years, the outgrowth of UCSD from the research traditions of Scripps, UCSD's formative years during the sixties and seventies, and the new millennium of rapidly changing technologies and research breakthroughs.

The architectural tour consists of ten walking tours of campus neighborhoods, with a total of 110 buildings. Within each tour/chapter, texts for each building explain the architecture as well as the physical and historical context. Each tour/chapter includes a map that makes it easy to locate individual buildings.

While the introduction will inform all the tours, one can begin this book with any chapter. The ten chapters are organized as self-contained walking tours of university neighborhoods such as Scripps, Muir College, and University Center. Chapters are ordered to follow the campus layout, so that each tour is followed by a tour of a nearby neighborhood. Where possible, tours begin or end with a special building or place: an example of particularly noteworthy architecture, a grand public space, a public art piece, or a convenient place to stop for a break or a meal.

Visitors are welcome to tour the UCSD campus.

For general information, call 858-534-2230, or visit the university website: www.ucsd.edu.

Marye Anne Fox, Chancellor (2004–)

At UCSD, we understand the importance of having a dynamic and vibrant environment to enrich academic and interpersonal experiences, and to stimulate thought and discussion. Our campus and environment are thoughtfully designed to enhance and encourage the university's tradition of collaboration and innovation. Our students, faculty, staff, and researchers transcend traditional boundaries in science, arts, and the humanities, and work across disciplines and job descriptions to solve current global challenges and improve our world. These brilliant minds are the reason UCSD has become one of the nation's most accomplished research universities, widely acknowledged for its local impact, national influence, and global reach.

As the campus has transformed and grown over the last five decades, our architecture and buildings have received numerous design awards and have been lauded for their sustainable construction. Our new buildings are all designed to meet a LEED Silver Rating certification. They minimize the need for air conditioning and heat, ensuring comfort and creating the ideal environment for learning and working.

As new neighborhoods and buildings are erected to house classrooms, laboratories, offices, and students, open spaces for recreation and academic and social meetings are also carefully preserved and designed. Most recently, we created a downtown district in the heart of campus that serves as a community hub for our students, staff, and faculty, and a welcoming area for our alumni and community visitors.

I hope you enjoy learning more about UCSD's unique history and campus in this guidebook, and I invite you to visit us soon.

FOREWORD

Richard C. Atkinson, President Emeritus of the University of California (1995–2003) and Chancellor Emeritus of UCSD (1980–1995)

Soon after I became chancellor in 1980, UCSD embarked on a new wave of expansion. I knew that as we added colleges, hired new faculty, and more than doubled enrollment, smart planning and excellent architecture would be essential.

Before I arrived at UCSD, I had spent time on some spectacular campuses. I earned my undergraduate degree at the University of Chicago, where the architecture was stately English Gothic, and the city included those great Frank Lloyd Wright buildings. I taught at Stanford University from 1956 to 1975, on a majestic campus that was master planned by Frederick Law Olmsted (best known for designing New York City's Central Park in 1858). I also took three years away from Stanford to teach at the University of California, Los Angeles, yet another campus with a strong sense of place.

So when, as UCSD's new chancellor, I began to think about how we would grow, I imagined a place that would have its own distinctive identity. The physical campus would continue to reflect our commitment to quality and innovation. It would make the most of our spectacular location amid the eucalyptus trees, next to the Pacific Ocean. The buildings would take full advantage of our temperate climate, which lets us live outdoors even during winter months.

Long before my arrival, the university's founders had already accomplished some of the most difficult and important tasks. In the late 1950s, when distinguished scientist Roger Revelle led a regional effort to build upon the academic excellence of the Scripps Institution of Oceanography and establish a new, comprehensive University of California campus in San Diego, he focused on one criterion: this new university had to become globally important and distinctive. Determined to build a campus in La Jolla, Revelle overcame extraordinary political and budgetary hurdles. He engineered the acquisition of a spectacular site, rallied community support, and persuaded eminent scholars to join him to create one of the world's foremost institutions of higher education.

UCSD's earliest planners recognized that a university's reputation relies on its ability to attract great teachers and researchers as well as gifted students. They also recognized that a magnificent campus would be a compelling attraction in recruitment efforts. Even before the first campus buildings were completed, the campus was a magnet. Listen to the stories of those first faculty who visited from around the country to consider new careers here, and nearly all of them recount the wonders of stepping out of an airplane into summer weather (even in winter!) and wandering our parklike plateau for the first time.

In the five decades since it was established as a research university, UCSD has risen to international prominence more quickly than any other institution founded during this period. I feel privileged to have led UCSD for fifteen years, a period during which enrollment doubled, faculty increased by 50 percent, many distinctive buildings were completed, and our efforts were recognized with dozens of awards for both academic excellence and architectural innovation.

This new guidebook is a tribute to those first fifty years. Although the focus is on innovative planning and excellent architecture, this story has as its central theme the emergence of a world-renowned university and the intimate connections between the people that make this such a phenomenal place and the campus that brings us together as a community in our shared mission of academic excellence.

In a few hours spent wandering the campus of the University of California, San Diego, one can sample a century's worth of modern architecture by architects such as Irving Gill, Lloyd Ruocco, Robert Mosher, and Rob Quigley. From modest wood buildings to brutalist concrete structures and sleek designs in steel and glass, the university campus displays a broad spectrum of styles and materials. Underlying these variations in aesthetics and engineering are two prime forces that have shaped the campus's layout and its architecture: the topography—a coastal sandstone bluff covered with scrubby native plants and stands of old eucalyptus trees—and the university's ceaseless quest for innovation. Research breakthroughs have created an atmosphere of experimentation that also encourages innovative architecture. In the sixties and seventies, the campus's formative years, it seemed possible that buildings might eventually overwhelm the site's natural beauty. Since then, thoughtful planning has preserved nature as an essential asset in the campus's development.

The Jacobs School of Engineering is one example of the synergy between science and architecture at UCSD that is helping to shape a new generation of buildings. These buildings incorporate technological features ranging from sophisticated laboratory equipment to new "green" materials. They also provide spaces designed to encourage collaboration and creativity, such as floor plans that cause spontaneous collisions between researchers, private offices with calming garden views, and multimedia meeting rooms that provide groups of academics with brain-sparking environments.

The school is home to the California Institute for Telecommunications and Information Technology (Calit2), where interdisciplinary collaborations are revolutionizing everything from cell-phone and Internet technology to solar power and computer music. With all of that neural electricity crackling, it's no surprise that Atkinson Hall (2005), Calit2's new building, is as futuristic as the research taking place inside. Its spectacular forms and surfaces were designed by NBBJ after a series of meetings with an advisory committee of faculty and scientists during which the architects gained a deep understanding of Calit2's projects and needs.

Inside Atkinson Hall, researchers and artists require uninterrupted wireless connections, so the architects incorporated a variety of communications-friendly features including an exterior skin of Trespa, a composite material that lets communications waves slide through. Structural steel is used instead of concrete because it allows the structure to be permeated by wireless signals. Because of the importance of spontaneity in the creative process, Atkinson Hall has an open, flowing interior that choreographs frequent collisions between creative types, who sometimes fuse new combinations of ideas.

The emerging model for building design at UCSD is to create new structures that accommodate and express the dynamic, innovative work that takes place inside them. As a result, a new generation of charmingly idiosyncratic buildings is emerging on campus—idiosyncratic not necessarily because of an architect's desire to experiment with new forms, but because of his or her commitment to understanding how a building can serve the needs of its users and meet the university's goals for neighborhood planning and energy self-sufficiency.

Keeping in mind the influence of these two factors—the spectacular natural setting and the spirited quest for innovative ideas—one can dig deep into UCSD's intellectual and architectural history and learn how the university has evolved over the course of fifty years with this double-coiled DNA intact.

An Architectural Snapshot of UCSD
UCSD has examples of every phase of modern architecture in San Diego. Before tracing this modern lineage, though, it is worth noting that UCSD does *not* have a single example of the historical-revival styles prevalent at other University of California campuses (including Los Angeles and Berkeley), and at San Diego's two other major universities, the University of San Diego and San Diego State University.

John S. Galbraith, UCSD's chancellor from 1964 to 1968, surveys the fledgling university, 1965

*Irving Gill's laboratory building
at Scripps (known today as the
Old Scripps Building), 1914*

Timing and planning are two main reasons for the modernist aesthetic
that unifies the campus. Beginning with the first master plan produced
by architect and planner Robert Alexander in 1963 and the first buildings
designed in the sixties by Robert Mosher and others, there was never a
hint of anything except modern architecture. UCSD was founded at a time
when modern architecture was just hitting its prime in San Diego, where
for several decades many of the city's best architects (such as Richard Requa
and William Templeton Johnson) made their names with historical styles,
and where communities such as Rancho Santa Fe (in the twenties) and
Rancho Bernardo (in the sixties) were developed with a Mediterranean
architectural theme.

Another sign of modern architecture's new status in California came
with the publication in 1960 of Esther McCoy's landmark book *Five
California Architects*, which put the state's modernist movement on the
architectural map.[1] Famed San Diego modernist Irving Gill was one of
the five, and his inclusion marked a significant resurrection for a man
whose occupation was listed on his death certificate as "laborer" when he
died in 1936.

Scripps Institution of Oceanography, with its first building designed
by Gill and completed in 1910, developed significantly before the founding
of UCSD. Even so, its architecture also hews to the modernist line.
Scripps did not build much during the twenties, thirties, and forties,
and so it was not influenced by the heyday of San Diego's Mediterranean
revival.

Nearly a century ago, architect Bertram Goodhue launched San Diego's
infatuation with romantic Spanish architecture. Even though UCSD has
not been seduced by historical styles, it is relevant to mention Balboa Park,
San Diego's monument to the romance of Old World architecture. Gill
almost won the coveted job of designing buildings for the 1915 Panama-
California Exposition—for which Balboa Park was created. His proposal
called for his signature minimalist modern buildings. But he was aced at the
eleventh hour by Goodhue, a prominent New York architect who lobbied
successfully for the commission. When UCSD's new main library (known

today as Geisel Library) opened in 1970, UCSD had its first landmark building by a famous architect—William Pereira had made the cover of *Time* magazine in September 1963 as a visionary. Today, UCSD has a collection of buildings by San Diego architects (from Irving Gill in 1910 to Rob Quigley in 2007) as well as some of the best-known architects in the world (Arthur Erickson, Romaldo Giurgola, Charles Gwathmey, Charles Moore, Antoine Predock, and Moshe Safdie).

The buildings range from sixties precast concrete (Muir College) to brutalist concrete (Mandeville Center, the Center for Magnetic Recording Research) to light-filled, glass-walled structures (the Natatorium) made possible by the development of stronger, more pliable glass. There are rustic wood courtyard buildings (the International Center) and recent steel-and-glass buildings (the Natural Sciences Building, Atkinson Hall) that show how newer materials allow architects to experiment with forms, light, and space in dynamic new ways. Recent buildings (and those on the drawing board) also express a commitment to green design that has a significant impact on a building's appearance, such as the solar arrays atop Gilman and Hopkins parking structures, or new varieties of energy-conserving glass. It will be fascinating to see how modernism evolves at UCSD in the decades ahead.

In the Beginning
UCSD opened in 1960, but its philosophical and aesthetic roots reach back to the first decade of the twentieth century and the birth of the marine biology lab that would become Scripps Institution of Oceanography.

In 1903 the Marine Biological Association of San Diego opened a small lab in the boathouse at the Hotel del Coronado at the request of University of California, Berkeley zoologist William Ritter. He wanted to conduct summer marine research and San Diego was eager to accommodate such a renowned scientist. In 1904 the lab moved from the boathouse to a small, new laboratory at La Jolla Cove, about a mile down the coast from Scripps's current location. As research expanded, the association began to outgrow that space; in 1906 Ellen Browning Scripps made an endowment of $50,000 toward future expansion. Her brother E. W. Scripps, a newspaper tycoon, leaned on the City of San Diego to sell 170 oceanfront acres north of the cove to the Marine Biological Association for a much larger new lab. The land was acquired for $1,000. E. W. Scripps built a road from La Jolla to the site. Architect Irving Gill was hired, and the building opened in 1910—a radically modern design in concrete alone on a bluff by the Pacific Ocean. The catalytic connection between scientific ambition and architectural innovation was established.

TOP: *Irving Gill's Scripps lab, Scripps Pier, and cottages built by E. W. Scripps to house faculty and researchers, 1925*
BOTTOM: *Scripps Institution's first director, William Ritter, at home with his wife on the second floor of Irving Gill's lab building, 1910*

At the dawn of the twentieth century, San Diego was a tiny, unsophisticated town, especially when compared with California's two booming urban centers. In 1900, Los Angeles counted 102,479 residents and San Francisco, 342,782. They became the first sites for University of California campuses, in Berkeley (1868) and Los Angeles (1919). They were major American cities, with all the power, prestige, prosperity, and spirit that accompany that position.

Meanwhile, San Diego in 1900 had a population of 17,000. La Jolla had only 350 residents; it was a village of clapboard beach cottages with a population that swelled when wealthy easterners made seasonal visits to their affordable La Jolla vacation homes. An electric trolley carried weekend visitors into the village from San Diego neighborhoods to the south.

The coastal bluff now occupied by Scripps Institution of Oceanography was barren. San Diego would still be a virtual desert if not for imported water. The average annual rainfall is about ten inches, and San Diego County did not begin to build the infrastructure to import vast amounts of water from the Colorado River and Northern California until the forties. To those who are only familiar with the lush look of La Jolla today, the La

Jolla of historical photos is virtually unrecognizable. A bird's-eye view circa 1900 reveals a vacant land with a stubble of dry native plants stretching for miles.

While La Jolla was laid-back, it is not a stretch to characterize early 1900s San Diego as having been part of the Wild West, where adventurers arrived to stake a claim. Wild dreams just might come true in San Diego; wild dreams would also bring risk-takers to UCSD in the decades to follow. In downtown San Diego, the Stingaree district (now known as the Gaslamp Quarter) was full of romantic Victorian buildings including more than a handful of saloons. There were also prostitutes and opium dens, outlaws and opportunists. Entrepreneur/gambler/buffalo hunter/law enforcer Wyatt Earp and his wife, Josie, for instance, owned or leased four Stingaree hotels and gambling halls between 1885 and 1887.

Ritter, the marine biologist from Berkeley, was already making research voyages along California's coast in the 1890s. He arrived in San Diego in 1903 to begin research supported by the Marine Biological Association. By 1910, he had been installed as the association's director, living on the second floor of the institution's first building (designed by Irving Gill and known today as the Old Scripps Building) and investigating the ocean waters near La Jolla. In 1912 the Marine Biological Association became part of the University of California and was renamed Scripps Institution of Biological Research. At this point, Scripps consisted of Gill's lab building and a few beach cottages built by E. W. Scripps to house the scientists. In 1913 Ritter moved to the house now known as the Old Director's House.

As the main UCSD campus up the hill evolved through various master plans over the years, Scripps Institution of Oceanography (renamed in 1925) continued on its own parallel track of development.

Launching a New University
Writers such as John Steinbeck, Upton Sinclair, and Kevin Starr have depicted California's coast as a fantasyland at the edge of the continent. California, the story goes, is a young culture with a short modern history, few traditions, wide-open spaces, and a spirit that anything is possible. In Steinbeck's *The Grapes of Wrath* (1939) or Sinclair's *Oil!* (1927) or Starr's authoritative California history series (1973–2009), the Golden State is a place where one can invent a new life from scratch. So is UCSD. Faculty and students come to the university from around the world and find, after a time, that their lives have changed completely.

But of course, California has a meaningful history prior to the twentieth century. Thousands of years before the arrival of UCSD and "civilization" in La Jolla, the Kumeyaay people were the native residents of Southern

Camp Matthews, 1950s

California. Archaeologists have discovered burial grounds, human bones, middens (domestic-waste disposal areas), and living areas on the site of the UCSD campus. The Kumeyaay lived in shelters built from willow, oak, manzanita, and other plant materials. They made baskets and pottery from indigenous plants and clay soil. They wore clothes crafted from the skins of rabbits, deer, and sea otters, shoes of agave or yucca fiber, and necklaces and bracelets of bones, claws, hooves, and shells. They shaped knives and weapons from stone, and they hunted rabbits, birds, and deer, and gathered roots, berries, nuts, and seeds from native plants. The arrival of European missionaries and explorers beginning in the seventeenth century eventually meant the end of the Kumeyaay way of life. Their land was taken away and used for missions and ranches where they were used as slave laborers. The newcomers brought diseases to which the Kumeyaay had no immunities. Sickness and violence killed a significant number of the population. Today, the Kumeyaay have once again become a force in the region as the proprietors of huge gaming resorts.

Meanwhile, war brought another identity to the vast acreage that would become UCSD. Gunshots ricocheted on Torrey Pines Mesa beginning in 1915, when the U.S. Marine Corps opened a firing range called Camp Matthews on 544 acres leased from the City of San Diego. By 1917, a Marine tent city had been added. The base expanded during World War II, and in 1943, at the height of the war, 100,000 marksmen went through training here—9,000 of them every three weeks. In addition to barracks, rifle ranges, and offices, Camp Matthews had a swimming pool, an outdoor theater, and a bowling alley (later home to UCSD's Center for Research in Computing and the Arts).

Camp Callan, 1945

Across Torrey Pines Road to the north, at Camp Callan, soldiers began training on large antiaircraft guns in 1940 to prepare to defend California's coast from enemy attacks. By 1943 ten thousand soldiers were stationed there, and the base included 297 buildings including barracks, three theaters, five chapels, offices, a 910-bed hospital, small-arms training ranges, and artillery stations guarding the coastline. The camp's seven-hundred-acre site is now occupied by Torrey Pines Golf Course, research facilities, Torrey Pines Glider Port, and UCSD buildings. It is virtually unrecognizable as the same place shown on a postcard from those times, where Camp Callan looks like a complete military city by the sea.

In the years following World War II, San Diego entered an era of expansion that would support a university. The region's population grew from 556,808 in 1950 to 1,033,011 in 1960. Economic growth was fueled by the Cold War explosion in defense spending. Decades earlier, San Diego had positioned itself as a military hot spot. Civic leaders wined and dined President Theodore Roosevelt in an attempt to convince him to shift the Navy's Pacific Fleet to San Diego. A few years later, while Franklin Roosevelt was Assistant Secretary of the Navy under President Woodrow Wilson, he received the same sort of pitch. By 1922 the Pacific Fleet's home port was the San Diego Naval Base just south of downtown, and today more than fifty Navy ships are based in San Diego. San Diego's fortunes soared with new military business, with UCSD's fortunes along for the ride. Much of the research at Scripps Institution of Oceanography has been defense-related. A significant number of UCSD's founding faculty came from work in the military or defense industries—some of them even helped create atomic weapons.

The most important figure in UCSD's early history, Roger Revelle, had a career closely tied to the military. Revelle earned bachelor's and master's degrees in geology at UC Berkeley. His association with Scripps Institution of Oceanography was twofold. In 1931, he married Ellen Scripps, whose great aunt was Ellen Browning Scripps. By one account, a check from the elder Ellen helped the newlyweds purchase the Chrysler convertible they piloted to La Jolla after their wedding in Pasadena. When they arrived, Revelle began his career at Scripps Institution of Oceanography.

From early on Revelle saw the potential of hitching one's fortunes to the military. In *Roger: A Biography of Roger Revelle*, authors Judith and Neil Morgan describe his first training cruise to Alaska with a fleet of Navy vessels: "It was his first glimpse of the Navy at work, and he quickly sensed that the new science of oceanography might be of lasting interest to the Navy."[2] Revelle joined the Navy Reserve during World War II and helped develop sonar equipment for detecting enemy submarines. At Scripps he set up a division called the Marine Physical Laboratory, devoted to Naval research, and Scripps soon landed a contract worth $175,000 a year. To quote Humphrey Bogart's famous line from *Casablanca* (1942), "I think this is the beginning of a beautiful friendship." From that point forward, numerous secret military research projects were transferred to Scripps. For example, Revelle led a team that gathered oceanographic data from the 1945 atomic bomb test site in the Bikini Atoll (a tiny cluster of Islands in the Pacific Ocean between California and Asia) and he returned in 1952 to measure the effects of a thermonuclear bomb explosion.

As Scripps grew into a world-renowned center for science, Revelle set out to bring a University of California campus to La Jolla. Always the entrepreneur, he could see the benefits of a first-rate science and engineering research university that could provide essential research and brainpower to science- and technology-related industries.

John Jay Hopkins, president of General Dynamics in the fifties, began planning a new lab building on Torrey Pines Mesa. (General Dynamics was best known for its ICBMs [Intercontinental Ballistic Missiles].) Hopkins was among those in the private sector lobbying for a new University of California campus, a think tank that would provide fresh ideas and talent to local industry. To broaden the university's appeal to the San Diego and La Jolla communities, Revelle proposed that the new campus also include facilities for La Jolla Playhouse, a theater company founded in 1947 by Gregory Peck, Mel Ferrer, and Dorothy McGuire. This seed of the arts at UCSD has since grown into a comprehensive, highly regarded collection of arts programs, including theatre and dance, music, visual arts, and literature.

But there was still one looming obstacle to a new university: in the late fifties and early sixties, La Jolla realtors and residents operated under an unspoken "covenant" that those of Jewish descent were not allowed to buy homes there. Besides being blatantly discriminatory, the covenant had already affected Scripps Institution's ability to attract top talent. In 1951, Revelle brought together a group of investors to purchase land near Scripps in a new development known as The Estates, with the plan that they would in turn sell lots at reasonable prices and with no restrictions. But launching a new university forced Revelle to find a permanent solution. Revelle was determined to break the covenant. Drawing on his strong ties within the community, he lobbied La Jolla civic leaders and real estate agents; he let them know that if the covenant remained, there would be no UCSD. Realtors understood the economic implications of having a significant new group of financially qualified buyers. By the time the university opened, the covenant had been broken.

In 1955 the City of San Diego offered land to the University of California at no cost. The university Board of Regents voted in 1956 to build a new campus in San Diego. The university received nearly 1,000 acres of city land in 1959—about 450 acres of the former Camp Callan plus the 545-acre Camp Matthews—for the new campus. The campus site was a scrubby expanse cut by canyons, with a large grove of old eucalyptus trees in plantation-style rows and dozens of old military buildings, some of which would become "staging areas" where new colleges would be housed as they began operations before their buildings were ready. Revelle envisioned a university that would eventually include a dozen small colleges. In 1960, UCSD was born with the establishment of a graduate institute of Science and Engineering. Los Angeles architect Stanley Gould of Risley and Gould designed four buildings (Bonner Hall, Urey Hall, Mayer Hall, and the Central Utilities Plant). Construction began in 1961.

Long-Range Planning at UCSD

Over the years, there have been five long-range development plans for the UCSD campus: in 1963, 1966, 1981, 1989, and 2004. In between each planning effort, a variety of factors influenced the campus's actual development: the ups and downs of state and university budgets, and changes in administration that brought different philosophies of campus growth and planning. Each new generation of design and planning professionals hired by the university to design new buildings and surrounding spaces brought to the table new approaches to planning, architecture, landscape design and the choice of plant materials, and the form and scale of public spaces. Each new long-range plan took into account this ever-evolving context.

TOP: *Robert Alexander's 1963 Master Plan, with its pedestrian "Champs Elysées"*
BOTTOM: *Revelle College, 1968*

In 1963 Los Angeles architect Robert Alexander was hired as UCSD's Consulting Architect, to prepare the first master plan for the entire 1,000-acre campus. Alexander's master plan configured twelve colleges as "jewels strung together on a necklace of promenades."[3] Colleges would each have a distinctive identity, and would be clustered in groups of four. Each college of 2,300 students would include

Roger Revelle speaks at Revelle College dedication, 1965

housing and recreational fields located at the perimeter, and would be organized around a central courtyard.

The campus's focal point would be a wide tree-lined "Champs Elysées" pedestrian boulevard that would run north-south along the western edge of campus. Anchoring the mall's midpoint (about where Thurgood Marshall College is today) would be the heart of the university: a 600-by-700-foot plaza "rivaling the Piazza San Marco" (where Ridge Walk is today). In the plaza a 360-foot communications/bell tower would sprout from the center of a 6,000-seat amphitheater, and there would be a library "as compelling as a Mayan Pyramid."[4] The university's administrative offices would also be in this campus center, as well as an auditorium, a theater-arts center, an art gallery/museum, and a TV and radio center.

The first phase of Alexander's plan was the construction of Revelle College, at the south end of his planned Champs Elysées. The vast scale of Revelle Plaza—not even as large as the grand piazza he had in mind for the center of campus—gives an idea of his scheme's monumentality. The size of the plaza is impressive, as seen in photos of it packed with student protesters during the sixties. Revelle College (named in honor of Roger Revelle) opened in 1964 with an initial class of 181.

Muir College came next, and it bears no similarity to Revelle. As planning for Muir College gained momentum in 1965 (it was founded in 1967), San Diego architect Robert Mosher, who was designing the new college's Applied Physics and Mathematics Building (1969), questioned Alexander's plan.[5] Mosher had studied architecture with Frank Lloyd Wright at Wright's Taliesin architecture school in Wisconsin, and he believed in a humanistic approach to planning and architecture. He felt that the vast scale of public spaces and buildings proposed by Alexander would be impersonal and overbearing, and that such a scheme would not suit the pristine natural context, nor would it create a serene and inspiring environment for contemplation and creativity. Recalling the university's early planning, Mosher compared Alexander's plan to the designs employed by dictators like Hitler and Mussolini to assert their power. He feared that students in the sixties, many of whom began mistrusting government, institutions, national leaders, and authority in general, might also make this kind of association. At UC Berkeley in 1965, public protests against the Vietnam War and the university administration attracted thousands. Likewise, students at UCSD filled Revelle Plaza for protests. The plaza can accommodate a crowd of thousands, and it's the only public space of its size in the heart of a UCSD college. But when it is not full of people, it can be perceived as a stark and impersonal expanse of space. Mosher, in thinking about what Muir College would be like, imagined that a more intimate plan would help connect students, administration, and faculty. He expressed his concerns to Alexander over lunch.[6] Alexander, Mosher says, asserted his authority (although Mosher didn't exactly put it that way). As UCSD's official master planner and architect, Alexander had drafted a plan with the university's guidance. It was intended to guide the campus's growth for years to come. But the administration, with prompting from some architects, would turn away from Alexander's plan after only one college had been completed.

Muir College, 1960s

Geisel Library and Muir College, 1970s

In 1964 John S. Galbraith became UCSD's second chancellor, replacing Herbert F. York. Galbraith recruited John Stewart from Dartmouth College as provost of Muir College. Stewart had double-majored in English and music at Ohio's Denison University and earned his doctorate in English literature at Ohio State University. Stewart's passion for the arts gave him an intuitive understanding of how people respond to buildings and public spaces. Mosher recalls meeting Stewart to express his concerns over Alexander's plan, and Mosher says that Stewart agreed with his criticisms. According to Mosher, he and Stewart joined several administrators for a brainstorming retreat at Warner Hot Springs, about an hour's drive east from San Diego. Mosher explained his objections, and, he says, the group agreed with many of his ideas about the value of creating a more intimate plan for Muir College, with smaller buildings and public spaces connected by gardens and courtyards. Mosher's lobbying for a more people-friendly approach, together with a new proposal as to where the university's new central library should be situated, would soon cause the university to part ways with Alexander and his master plan.

In 1965, Los Angeles architect William Pereira—an early "starchitect" who made the cover of *Time* magazine in 1963—was hired to design UCSD's new main library. Pereira felt the library should be built in the center of campus, not in Alexander's grand piazza at the far western edge. The university accepted his recommendation, and, following such a drastic change to his plan, Alexander resigned. To replace him as consulting architect, UCSD appointed A. Quincy Jones. Given Pereira's sway with the

UCSD administration, Jones's appointment had a political aspect: Five years earlier, Jones and Pereira had collaborated with great success on a master plan for the city of Irvine, an hour north of San Diego. Pereira was building consensus at UCSD. Jones delivered a new, drastically different plan in 1966:

> In addition to relocating the campus core (now called University Center), and the central library with it, it appears to have eliminated (or ignored) Alexander's north-south promenade on the old highway 101 ridge [along the west side of campus]. This is noteworthy because the Mandeville Center, designed by Jones, is a significant encroachment on this grand north-south mall, envisioned by Alexander to stretch from Revelle College to the north campus.[7]

It is surprising that Alexander and Jones ended up as polar opposites at UCSD, as they had had similar career tracks in Los Angeles. Both were dedicated modernists who had been recognized for their thoughtful planning. Alexander's best-known project is the Village Green, an affordable housing project near Los Angeles completed in 1945 that was notable for relegating cars to the periphery, and for its inviting, pedestrian-oriented landscape. This does not sound like the Alexander who worked for UCSD. Jones is remembered for his innovative residential architecture, and he was one of the first to incorporate greenbelts in tract-housing plans. At UCSD he proved that his reputation was no fluke.

In his new plan Jones retained Alexander's twelve colleges in three clusters. He eliminated the monumental plaza and tower, and moved the library to Pereira's preferred location. Jones also scrapped a proposed road through the center of campus and added pedestrian paths in a more organic pattern influenced by the natural terrain. While Mosher completed the design of the Applied Physics & Mathematics Building (1969), Jones gave the Muir College plan a complete overhaul. As opposed to Alexander's idea of massive towers around a big plaza, it became an intimate neighborhood of smaller buildings connected by landscaped walkways and courtyards. With Muir College finally underway, efforts shifted to UCSD's Third College, which opened in 1970 and was renamed Thurgood Marshall College in 1993.

When Marshall College was created at the height of the sixties, African American, Mexican American, and Native American students seized the opportunity to have a voice in a university with a predominantly white student body and a curriculum that emphasized a Eurocentric view of history. Controversial UCSD faculty member Herbert Marcuse, a Marxist philosopher and political theorist, became a prominent spokesman for the student cause, as did his articulate graduate student, budding African American activist Angela Davis. Marcuse was a critic of American government in general and the University of California administration in particular. By the time Marshall College opened in 1970, it incorporated many of the demands for a broad, multicultural curriculum. The campus was conceived as an intimate cluster of low buildings that might create the sense of a shared mission apart from other UCSD colleges. The Marshall campus provides a wide range of spaces: classrooms, offices, labs, and lecture halls, connected by indoor and outdoor public spaces including balconies, courtyards, and rolling lawns.

Marshall College was planned by Los Angeles architects Kennard and Silvers, which also designed virtually all of the college's buildings. The college was built during a time of tight budgets, but at the same time, the selection of courses had been expanded to meet the demand for a broader, multicultural curriculum. As a result, the college built a variety of spaces, utilizing basic materials such as stucco, plain doors and railings, and simple windows, with no funds for details, stone trim, hardwood flooring, and more elaborate forms that can be found at other UCSD colleges. But as is true throughout the UCSD campus, it's the planning of spaces between buildings that creates a sense of place. The planning of Marshall College is very effective in this regard. Buildings, paths, plazas, and courtyards do not align with the prevalent UCSD campus grid. As a result, even on a budget, the neighborhood features a dynamic array of spaces. Today, with a mature landscape, it is lush and inviting.

By the time Marshall opened in 1970, UCSD had survived its first decade to stake its claim as a credible university within the University of California system. UCSD had become a desirable choice for students, and it was earning recognition for graduate programs in engineering, the sciences, and music. As UCSD continued to evolve, development efforts shifted to the east, and the campus entered a new phase of growth.

UCSD Comes of Age

When the spaceship-like Central Library (now known as Geisel Library) opened in 1970, in the central campus location proposed by Pereira, the university had taken the first step toward building the busy center that would establish its mature identity. With its spectacular design, the new library was a much more suitable and attractive icon than Alexander's proposed 360-foot tower. The library is so distinctive that its silhouette was adopted as the university's official logo.

The university's architectural growth slowed during the seventies and early eighties. Compared with the booming launch of the sixties and the bigger boom that came during the nineties and the first decade of the new millennium, the seventies and eighties brought comparatively few new buildings. During the lull the focus shifted to academic evolution—as opposed to new construction—giving planners time to consider the successes and failures of development to date.

Warren College, the university's fourth, was founded in 1974 and temporarily housed in the Camp Matthews "staging area" of old military buildings, where earlier UCSD colleges had also begun. The first new buildings for Warren did not arrive until the late eighties, and most of them, especially for the Jacobs School of Engineering, were constructed in the nineties and in the last decade.

The Warren campus runs east from Geisel Library. Buildings line a landscaped pedestrian mall of patterned concrete, grass, and landscaped seating areas. The new college brought a new wave of concrete buildings, more stark than the concrete buildings at Muir and Revelle colleges, also more striking with their plain, bold forms. In many cases, the buildings of Warren College are also more open and inviting at the ground level. Buildings such as the Center for Magnetic Recording Research (1986) and the Engineering Building Unit I (1990) are examples of the second wave of concrete buildings at UCSD.

Meanwhile, UCSD's third Long-Range Development Plan was finished in 1981, an update of Jones's 1966 long-range plan. Unlike previous and subsequent plans, the 1981 plan was not drafted by an outside consultant such as Alexander or Jones. Instead, "it was under the purview of the lay Campus/Community Planning Committee.... As the state capital budget for the university was almost non-existent during this period, physical development became opportunistic [often funded by outside donations] and the idea of adhering to a coherent plan seemed irrelevant. (Besides, the 1981 plan was so general that almost anything adhered to it)."[8]

Fifth College was founded in 1988 and operated for several years in buildings scattered around campus. It was renamed Eleanor Roosevelt College in 1994, and moved to its own campus at UCSD in 2003.

In the late eighties, as UCSD headed for a new phase of expansion and construction, Nevada architect Boone Hellmann fortuitously arrived on the scene. In 1985, Hellmann had sold his architectural practice in Reno and moved to San Diego with the intention of earning a law degree to specialize in construction litigation. Meanwhile, to cover his expenses, he took a job as a project manager in UCSD's Office of Facilities Design and Construction. As Hellmann recalls,

> I soon discovered that the university was a very interesting place and
> I could sense an entrepreneurial spirit that I had never experienced in
> an academic setting. Chancellor Richard Atkinson, Vice Chancellor—

Administration V. Wayne Kennedy, and Vice Chancellor—Resource Management and Planning John Woods were three of the most dynamic, forward-thinking, "we can do it" individuals I have ever met. I began to get excited about the plans they had for UCSD.[9]

In 1987 Hellmann was appointed Campus Architect. At the same time, campus faculty and administrative leaders decided it was time to develop a comprehensive, updated master plan, since the academic, demographic, and economic assumptions that guided the initial plans were no longer valid. Consequently, a group of faculty and administrative leaders defined a new set of planning objectives and selected a team of consultants led by Professor Richard Bender (formerly dean of the School of Architecture and Environmental Design at UC Berkeley) in partnership with Skidmore, Owings & Merrill (SOM) to develop the new plan. Throughout the planning process, UCSD's dedicated team worked closely with the professional planners.[10]

The 1989 UCSD Master Plan Study is exceptionally lucid and concise. It defines succinct guidelines for future growth. Instead of the initial 1963 plan for twelve colleges of 2,300 students, the objective became to create up to eight colleges of 2,500 undergraduates in each, plus capacity for 7,500 graduate students not associated with a college. In the university's first fifty years, the plan stands as the definitive planning document. It takes stock of the state of campus, from planning and architecture, to public space, open space, and natural resources including eucalyptus trees and endangered species. It sets simple guidelines for future growth that will preserve and enhance the campus's character.

> [The plan is] underlain by two linked fundamental characteristics. First, it is an environmentally-based plan. It was prepared by first identifying land unsuitable for development for reasons of environmental sensitivity, then planning new development on what was left. It departs from its antecedents in its emphasis on stewardship of the land—the importance of preserving and cherishing the unique physical qualities of the campus setting and environment. Second, the Plan adopts the view that the primary role of all buildings is to generate a coherent and beautiful network of open spaces; the emphasis is on common space created by careful placement of buildings, instead of buildings themselves. This second characteristic is the key element distinguishing America's most physically revered campuses.[11]

The plan is built around five themes: Neighborhoods, University Center, Academic Corridors, The UCSD Park, and Connections.

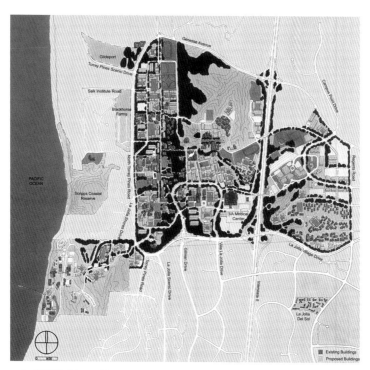

1989 UCSD Master Plan

As Alexander's plan did, the 1989 plan emphasizes the importance of creating campus neighborhoods: "Each college should be distinct but internally unified.... Each neighborhood is to have a distinct character growing out of a unified pattern of buildings and open spaces, with a unified architectural thread. Five Academic Corridors will consist of walkways and gathering areas that cut across neighborhood boundaries to bring related academic departments together by discipline."[12] Connections are walkways, bicycle paths, landmarks, view corridors, transit systems, and other elements that link the campus together. It is essential that they "function as a unified whole" that glues the campus together. Vast improvements have been made in support of this goal during the past twenty or thirty years. Where once it was easy to get lost trying to get from one place to another—even for those who knew the campus—now there are many interconnected routes. Throughout the campus, there is a sense of that intangible thing that planners, architects, and romantics refer to as "a sense of place."

Perhaps the most important element in the plan is University Center, an urban district around the Price Center (1993–2008). Unlike other college campuses like UC Berkeley or UCLA, UCSD is a suburban campus without the surrounding concentration of people that can make a place vibrant and exciting. The new urban district outlined in the 1989 plan remedies the situation with new buildings unlike any predecessors on campus. Four or five stories high, they line the edges of sidewalks like the buildings that can be found in thriving metropolitan areas. At the street level, wide openings lead inside or through the buildings to courtyards or gardens. The plan suggests that buildings also include ground-floor retail spaces to help keep sidewalks busy.

Twenty years after the plan's completion, University Center is well on its way. As intended, it has become a popular destination. Additions to the Price Center include a new food court, a post office, a nightclub, a general store, an espresso café, and a variety of new public spaces with tables, chairs, and benches. The Price Center is to UCSD what Horton Plaza Shopping Center is to downtown San Diego: the centerpiece of a successful revitalization.

South of the Price Center, the Student Services Center helps energize the emerging urban district. A broad plaza runs beneath the building; around the perimeter, along busy sidewalks, are a copy center, a yogurt shop, and a restaurant. The lawn behind the building is a popular area that attracts people and provides places for them to sit, play, interact, and stay awhile. William Whyte, the renowned author and astute observer of people's behavior in public spaces, would tell us that this activity is a sign of successful planning. Even a parking lot makes a significant contribution to the urban fabric. Gilman Parking Structure (2002) does not look much like a parking structure. Thanks to some attractive design details, cars are barely visible, and the ground level includes a credit union and the university's parking office. Across the street, the Conrad Prebys Music Center (2008) has two wide entry plazas. At night, they are often filled with music lovers attending concerts, and the scene resembles a night out on the town.

A Landmark Collection of Public Art
UCSD has what is probably the most distinctive collection of public art on any American university campus. Beginning in 1983 with artist Niki de Saint Phalle's *Sun God*, the Stuart Collection has commissioned seventeen pieces, all of them responding to sites selected by the artists.[13] Terry Allen's *Talking Trees* (1986) blends into a eucalyptus grove, where it surprises people with music and poems and stories. On the day of President Barack Obama's inauguration, his speech could be heard emanating from the trees. San Diego artist Robert Irwin's *Two Running Violet V Forms* (1983) merges into another part of the grove, testing one's perceptions of space and light. Jackie Ferrara's *Terrace* is a landscaped addition to the Palade Laboratories for Cellular & Molecular Medicine, and Alexis Smith's *Snake Path* descends a slope to the east of the Geisel Library. Behind everything is Mary Beebe,

Barbara Kruger, Another, *2008, from the Stuart Collection*

who has served as the collection's director from the start. Beebe combines unerring judgment of art and artists with a vast knowledge of the field and an uncanny ability to convince even the most conservative bureaucrats of the merits of the most unimaginable projects. Only a few of the Stuart Collection's works are pictured in this book, but there is much more information available online, including detailed descriptions, photos, and a map.[14]

What Lies Ahead
Sixth College opened in 2002. Its first buildings include the Visual Arts Facility, Pepper Canyon Hall, and the Gilman Parking Structure—all mainstays of UCSD's emerging urban core. But new buildings at Sixth College represent only a fraction of the anticipated construction. By 2020 UCSD will nearly double the amount of building space on campus.

In 2004 the university provided a booster shot to the 1989 plan in the form of a Long-Range Development Plan (prepared by the UCSD Physical Planning Office in consultation with the Academic Senate, campus administrators, and the UC Office of the President) to guide UCSD's growth through 2020, when the campus is expected to have 29,900 students and a total population of 49,700—about the same as Loveland, Colorado; Cupertino, California; or Biloxi, Mississippi. As evidence of the 1989 plan's clear vision, the 2004 update makes no major changes, only clarifications that will help architects and planners make consistently sound decisions. It reiterates the same five themes: Neighborhoods, University Center, Academic Corridors, The UCSD Park, and Connections. It reinforces and expands the importance of preserving and restoring natural habitat.

Neighborhoods are defined in greater detail as "compact clusters of buildings, courts, plazas, quadrangles, and open spaces, and have distinct boundaries and entries. Each neighborhood should follow specific architectural and landscape design guidelines, and landscaping and the siting and massing of buildings within a neighborhood will preserve view corridors for the campus and community whenever possible."[5] But it is difficult to imagine how this will work. Eleanor Roosevelt College looks distinctive yet unified because architect Moshe Safdie planned the campus and designed all of the buildings. At other UCSD colleges, architects may not be eager to adhere to the themes.

On the other hand, University Center is an excellent example of how the Neighborhoods concept can succeed. Here is a cluster of buildings by a variety of leading architects. While each building has its own personality, each is also compatible with its neighbors because it uses similar proportions and materials and makes strong connections to the neighborhood.

Since Hellmann became campus architect more than twenty years ago, he has improved the quality of architecture and enhanced the university's reputation by hiring some of the best architects in the world, including several San Diego firms that have started to earn the same kinds of international awards, recognition, and media coverage as their prominent out-of-town peers. Decades ago, when San Diego was small and run by a sort of "old boy network," it was thought that one did not need to look outside the city for a good architect. Since then, San Diego has grown up. Many of its architects have reputations that reach far beyond the city limits. And as the city has become known internationally as a great place to live, with a redeveloped downtown that is a model of good planning, architects from around the world are eager to design buildings at UCSD.

In 2010, California is emerging from an economic downturn that cut University of California budgets and froze new construction. Historically, though, California always bounces back. Meanwhile, a new lull gives UCSD another opportunity to take stock of the most recent building boom and make adjustments for the next wave of growth. Just ahead are new sources of funding, new research…and new buildings.

WALK ONE: SCRIPPS INSTITUTION OF OCEANOGRAPHY

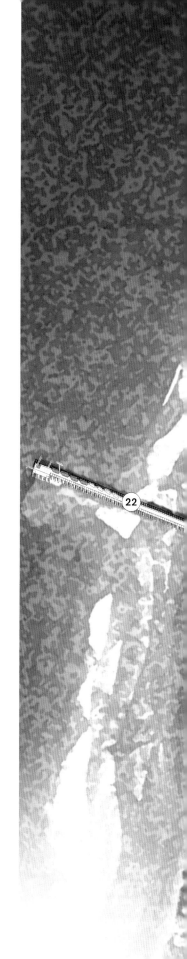

Coast Apartments

1. Coast Apartments
Mosher Drew Watson & Ferguson, 1969

Graduate students live at the top of the university's student food chain, so when it comes to campus housing, they choose from some of the best. In a clearing in a eucalyptus grove west of the main UCSD campus, the Coast Apartments are 106 units in a dozen two-story buildings circling a broad lawn dotted with mature trees. The site is breathtaking: many apartments have spectacular ocean views.

Exterior walls are finished in wood and stucco. Metal awnings with horizontal fins shade second-level windows. Vertical steel grates and narrow steel handrails wrap staircases and balconies without blocking light and ocean views. Low concrete-block walls or chest-high wood fences define individual patios for each first-floor apartment. Patios and balconies on the side of each building that faces the central lawn have views of other patios and balconies across the lawn, encouraging natural and frequent interaction between students.

Rolling lawns, serpentine sidewalks, and wide landscaped beds around buildings add to the sense of a secluded retreat from campus. There is more open space here than at most campus housing at UCSD. Buildings are several yards apart, and the lawn is roughly the size of a football field. Evergreen and deciduous trees ranging from eucalyptuses to pines, palms, and liquidambars create a constantly changing panorama of light, shadow, and color. Most days, the trees whisper as they sway with persistent ocean breezes.

While undergrads living on campus mostly eat at student dining halls, the graduate students at Coast Apartments have kitchens, which adds a familial, domestic vibe to the neighborhood. Wetsuits, surfboards, and bicycles can be seen on many decks and balconies. The Pacific Ocean is within walking or biking distance (although the climb back up La Jolla Shores Drive requires decent lungpower). For racqueteers, an oceanview tennis court across the street from Coast Apartments is surprisingly available—it is not well known to the campus and public.

Coast Apartments opened in 1969, a memorable year in American history. Neil Armstrong's first steps on the moon (July 16) and the Woodstock Music & Arts Festival (August 15 to 19) made headlines only weeks apart that summer. While some buildings completed in that era are beginning to show their age, the Coast Apartments, with their clean lines, durable and decorative steel awnings and railings, and thoughtful landscaping now fully grown, may look even better today than they did the day they opened.

2. UCSD Park

Wandering the walkways, roads, and steep stairs that wind through the Scripps Institution of Oceanography campus, it is impressive to note how much the campus— and UCSD in general—have grown over the past century without ruining the inherent natural beauty of the university's prime coastal property. The UCSD Park concept was set forth in the 1989 UCSD Master Plan.[1] In 2004, as part of a new fifteen-year Long-Range Development Plan (LRDP), campus planners emphasized three priorities for maintaining and enhancing the natural environment. These three elements— the Ecological Reserve, the Grove Reserve, and Restoration Lands—are known collectively as UCSD Park.[2] The Ecological Reserve consists of canyons and other biologically sensitive areas preserved in perpetuity, with no construction permitted. The Grove Reserve refers primarily to the campus's old stands of eucalyptus, which have become iconic features of the campus. Future expansion is restricted here, and "wherever possible, efforts should be made to eliminate buildings and restore the eucalyptus groves." Restoration Lands are slopes, canyons, and coastal bluffs damaged by erosion, invasive vegetation, and past military uses.[3] The LRDP spells out restoration measures. Development may occur in some areas provided it has an "acceptable" impact. One area that will require special attention is Pepper Canyon, just west of Interstate 5, at the eastern edge of the main campus, where future plans include a light-rail transit station.

UCSD Park

Twenty-five years earlier, plans to preserve natural resources—particularly the eucalyptus trees—might have sounded like gibberish to architect Robert Alexander, author of the first UCSD master plan. "The Alexander plan showed little regard for the campus' eucalyptus groves and stands of native vegetation," observes the *UCSD Master Plan Study and its Antecedents*.[4] "While the plan did not propose wholesale filling of canyons, it saw them as convenient places to place parking garages."

By the time work began on the 1989 plan, the campus had added dozens of new buildings. Meanwhile, there was growing awareness on campus of the importance of preserving natural resources. A turning point came during the late eighties, when hundreds of eucalyptuses were cut down to make way for the Price Center. When they discovered the glaring expanse of stumps that remained, students made a public display of their anger: "White crosses were stapled to the trunks and toy bulldozers were placed in cages among them," recounts the 1995 *Master Plan Study and its Antecedents*. "Never again would campus administrators ignore the power of these trees in the campus psyche."[5]

Fast forward fifteen years: The LRDP of 2004, with its "Park at UCSD" section, provides specific guidelines to maintain and even enhance the natural beauty of UCSD's prime coastal acreage. After all, the campus's raw beauty provides daily enjoyment to the UCSD population; serves as an important feature in recruitment (dating back to Roger Revelle's early efforts during the late fifties and early sixties); and represents a significant piece of Southern California's natural habitat.

3. Birch Aquarium

Wheeler Wimer Blackman and Associates, 1992

Live fish and other sea creatures had been on view at the Scripps Institution of Oceanography for decades, but never in a world-class facility until Birch Aquarium's opening. It is the public face of Scripps Institution, a user-friendly museum, where visitors explore the underwater world of the Southern California coast and learn about some of the threats to this natural habitat.

From the parking lot to the galleries, the peach-and-aqua stucco building is friendly and welcoming. Two bronze whales leap from a circular pool in front of the building. A colorful mural of an underwater scene is painted on a fence. Starfish bearing the names of donors decorate a stucco wall in the entry courtyard. Two gigantic translucent seahorses adorn the glass walls flanking the main entrance.

The tall atrium lobby features a slanted ceiling and a view through a wall of glass to a broad terrace with an ocean view. A shark jawbone and several authentically preserved sharks hang overhead in the lobby. In one corner, a school of small silver fish swirls in a cylindrical tank.

Stephen Birch Aquarium

Galleries include tanks in many shapes and sizes with overhead skylights filtering daylight dreamily through water, sea life, and kelp beds. The spaces, which flow smoothly from one to another, also feature photos, models, videos, illustrations, historical timelines, and explanatory texts that help visitors to understand the marine species and habitats on view. Galleries are wide enough to handle large crowds, with exhibitions designed to keep people moving through the spaces.

The mission of Birch Aquarium is "to provide ocean science education, to interpret Scripps research, to promote ocean conservation."[6] Interaction is the key to engaging visitors, especially children who visit with families or school groups. Bold, colorful graphics, easy-to-understand texts, and displays that are not too high are all features that make Birch Aquarium a great place for children. The aquarium also provides kid-friendly ways to combine learning with fun and games. Child-size display tanks ask them, "How many potbellied seahorses can you find"? and "Can you find the frogfish?" Low tables have paper, pens, glue, and other materials young visitors use to depict the sea life they learn about at the museum. In the courtyard, plastic basins filled with small, harmless sea creatures serve as an aquatic petting zoo.

The aquarium's roots reach back to the early history of Scripps. In 1905, the marine lab for the Marine Biological Association of San Diego—Scripps's predecessor—occupied a small building at La Jolla Cove and was open to the public, but it was a working laboratory that was not designed as a public attraction. In 1910, Scripps moved to its first building on the current 170-acre campus. Designed by Irving Gill, it is known today as the Old Scripps Building. When it opened, the Gill building included a first-floor aquarium and a second-level marine museum. In 1915 Scripps opened a new aquarium in a 24-by-48-foot wood building with tanks that held up to 228 gallons of water (a typical bathtub holds 20 to 40 gallons). Curator Percy Barnhart filled the tanks with specimens he caught himself off Scripps Pier. Barnhart also displayed realistically painted plaster casts of fish, a variety of shells, and various stuffed fish.

Sam Hinton, Barnhart's successor, served as aquarium curator for thirty years (he also become a well-known folk singer). Hinton helped design the three-story Thomas Wayland Vaughan Aquarium Museum (named in honor of the institution's second director, who followed founding director William Ritter). It opened in 1951 and featured eighteen tanks of half-inch-thick Herculite tempered glass sealed in metal frames with special glue and rubberized cork gaskets. The tanks held as much as two thousand gallons of water. The Vaughan Aquarium was demolished years ago.

Thanks to Hinton, it was a wildly colorful place that attracted two hundred thousand visitors a year. Concrete walls and floors of tanks were painted turquoise, light green, dark green, light blue, deep blue, maroon, gray, and black.[7] Earlier tanks at Scripps, intended for research and not for public viewing, were purely utilitarian and not colorful. Hinton hoped his tanks would capture some of the excitement of the underwater environment. While the annual budget at Birch Aquarium is about $140 million, Hinton's annual budget was less than $20,000, including $350 for fish food.

Scenic ocean-view terraces complete the experience at Birch Aquarium. After an hour or two spent watching sea creatures swim within inches of their noses, visitors have a new appreciation for the Pacific Ocean when they step out onto the terrace, look across that vast expanse of blue, and imagine what lives beneath its calm and mysterious surface.

4. Nierenberg Hall
Neptune and Thomas, 1984

With its opening, Nierenberg Hall marked the expansion of Scripps Institution of Oceanography to a site east of the original campus. Today this east-side property also includes the Keck Center and Spiess Hall, and has become an important satellite of the main Scripps campus. Nierenberg Hall occupies a plum of a site at the east end of the Scripps Crossing pedestrian bridge, perched a few hundred feet above sea level with sweeping views of the coastline.

Clad in gray wood siding, concrete, tan stucco, and sun-screening dark glass, the building consists of a four-story L-shaped structure distinguished by two circulation towers on opposite sides of the center courtyard in the west-facing crook of the L,

William A. Nierenberg Hall

connected to a one-story L-shaped wing to the south. On the building's north end, horizontal rows of windows are flush with horizontal sections of wood siding. On the west and south, though, the horizontal bands of wood project from the building to shade windows below them. The east side, overlooking the parking lot and access road, does not have many windows.

Tables and low concrete benches in the courtyard provide places for coffee or a sandwich high above the blue Pacific Ocean. A wide sundeck on the second floor overlooks the courtyard. The landscape consists of a broad lawn to the west (facing the ocean) and, around the building, a variety of trees and shrubs ranging from pines to palms and roses.

Nierenberg Hall is named for William A. Nierenberg, the fifth director of Scripps Institution of Oceanography from 1965 to 1986. Over the course of his career, Nierenberg's research ranged from sonar systems for detecting enemy submarines to nuclear weaponry (including the Manhattan Project). At Scripps, Nierenberg's work included the Deep Sea Drilling Project to explore ocean-floor sediments, as well as probing the impact of oceans on atmospheric temperature, weather, and other aspects of the environment.

Under Nierenberg's leadership, Scripps expanded its research to encompass many related scientific fields including physics, Nierenberg's specialty dating back to his graduate-school days at Columbia University.[8] As a result, Scripps moved from financial instability to stability as government and grant funds began to flow in. By the time Nierenberg departed, the institution was well into a new era of expansion that produced Nierenberg Hall and many subsequent buildings.

W. M. Keck Foundation Center for Ocean Atmosphere Research

5. Keck Center for Ocean Atmosphere Research
Barton Myers Associates, 1998

Inspired by San Diego's architectural heritage of connecting indoor and outdoor spaces and of coastal buildings of weathered wood, Barton Myers Associates designed the W. M. Keck Foundation Center for Ocean Atmosphere Research as a garden paradise consisting of a modest two-story wood structure arranged around a courtyard bursting with greenery.

The Keck OAR 1 is a research lab building that sits on an oceanview bluff east of La Jolla Shores Drive. From here, it is a scenic walk across the Scripps Crossing pedestrian bridge to the main Scripps Institution of Oceanography campus and La Jolla Shores beach.

Barton Myers Associates heeded the local context with a building that suits its oceanview site and its occupants: scientists who often head to the beach for lunch-hour surfing sessions. Weathered surfers seem to appreciate the weathered wood structures and sprawling, slightly unkempt garden—their surfboards and wetsuits look right at home leaning on walls and hanging from railings.

Framed in steel, redwood, and concrete, wrapped in wood shingles, and capped with a standing-seam metal roof, the Keck OAR 1 building surrounds its overgrown courtyard like a tree house in the treetops. Three wings surround the courtyard, which is open to the south. Three-story and two-story wings come together in an L. A third detached one-story wing runs along the edge of the parking lot.

Balconies and covered walkways run the length of each wing along the courtyard. Simple lattices of horizontal redwood strips shade these spaces. Heavy horizontal, vertical, and diagonal members are tied together by steel brackets with countersunk bolts exposed. Handrails are thin strips of steel with steel cables. The rugged hardware adds to the building's raw appeal.

A shaggy landscape completes the rustic design. The courtyard is surrounded by wide concrete steps and low concrete beds planted with bronze flax and other water-sippers. The courtyard landscape tends toward the tropical and includes banana and palm trees, kangaroo paw, agapanthus, statice, philodendron, and plumeria, producing a range of sizes, shapes, textures, green and yellow leaf tones, and vivid flowers. Taken all together, the building and landscape give the effect of a tropical island hideaway out of Robinson Crusoe—a fantastical place that helps researchers dream.

6. Scripps Crossing

Burkett and Wong Engineers, designed by Frieder Seible with Safdie Rabines Architects, 1994

Great bridges—the kind that people come to see from miles around—are few and far between. But Scripps Crossing gets that kind of attention. It is a pedestrian bridge over La Jolla Shores Drive that connects the upper campus and main campus of Scripps Institution of Oceanography. A walk (or wheelchair rise—newer UCSD buildings conform to the accessibility guidelines set forth in the federal Americans with Disabilities Act of 1992) across it provides one of San Diego's most sublime coastal views, including La Jolla Shores beach, Mount Soledad, the village of La Jolla, and a broad expanse of blue that is often occupied by surfers, swimmers, sailboats, fishing boats, kayaks, and just about any other aquatic conveyance one can imagine.

The bridge was designed by a seasoned team of bridge specialists, including UCSD engineer Frieder Seible (dean of the Jacobs School of Engineering), Burkett and Wong Engineers, and Safdie Rabines Architects. At UCSD's Powell Structural Systems Laboratory, Seible has supervised testing of components for major bridges including the new span of the San Francisco Bay Bridge.

Scripps Crossing is an integral part of the "Scripps Ladder" concept conceived by architect William Turnbull in the 1994 Hillside Neighborhood Planning Study for Scripps.[9] The ladder refers to a collection of interconnected paths, bridges, elevators, and open-air corridors that climb the steep hillside site.

Scripps Crossing is a 140-foot single-tower cable stayed bridge with a special twist to its suspension system. The tower is planted east of La Jolla Shores Road instead of in the middle—an arrangement that at first seems out of balance. Cables run west from the tower to the bridge deck. But to the east, the deck is not suspended from cables. Instead, it cantilevers across to rest on a concrete pier.

Meanwhile the cables, instead of attaching to the bridge deck, are anchored into the hillside to stabilize the tower.

The end result is light and graceful feat of engineering that strikes a balance between tension and support. Cables are encased in stainless steel sleeves. Railings are stainless steel, as is other hardware. In a certain light, the bridge takes on the luster of a fine bracelet.

Once you cross the bridge headed west, more drama awaits. From the top of the wood-and-steel elevator tower, the panoramic ocean vista spreads out like a perfect azure postcard. Step into the elevator and enjoy the floating sensation as the coastal view slides by.

7. Martin Johnson House

Architect unknown, 1915

The Martin Johnson House is a generic beach bungalow of a kind commonly found in Southern California a century ago, but besides being an example of vintage regional architecture, it is a vital place in the early legacy of Scripps Institution of Oceanography.

When E. W. Scripps committed his support to Scripps, he thought not only of science and laboratories, but also of creating a neighborhood where researchers could live and work by the ocean. Martin Wiggo Johnson had worked as a plank-tonologist and as curator of the Puget Sound Biological Station before he came to Scripps in 1932. Like many other Scripps employees, he rented one of the cottages built by Scripps. Johnson and his wife raised two children there. In 1982, after it had been renovated and reopened as a meeting and special events center, it was named in honor of Martin Johnson.

The house is just east of the footpath that snakes along the bluff through the upper portion of the Scripps campus. Covered with narrow horizontal wood siding, it features gabled roofs and large decks. Only yards from the bluff, the house's decks offer spectacular ocean views. The experience of being there is a rare phenomenon largely unique to California, combining a bit of Central California and High Sierra (the trees) with the moody coastal climate and views. Today the repurposed house serves as a conference room and a place for special events. Outdoor wedding receptions on the decks are especially popular.

Much of Johnson's work involved research cruises, including a hydrographic survey of the Gulf of California. During World War II, he worked at the University of California Division of War Research operated by Scripps on Point Loma in San Diego. He identified the "deep scattering layer" of underwater organisms that interfered with sonar transmissions used by the military to track enemy submarines. Johnson also coauthored the textbook *The Oceans: Their Physics, Chemistry and General Biology* (1942), which served as an essential textbook for several decades.

Scripps Crossing

TOP: *Martin Johnson House*
BOTTOM: *Walter and Judith Munk Laboratory for Geophysics*

8. Munk Laboratory

Lloyd Ruocco, 1963

In the forties, Lloyd Ruocco became San Diego's first important midcentury modern architect. Ruocco's innovative use of steel framing, glass walls, and open floor plans made him a pioneer among postwar modernists. Ruocco served as a mentor to many younger San Diego architects, many of who also designed buildings at UCSD. Ruocco began his career in a historical-revival mode, working for architect Richard Requa at a time when Requa was designing the Spanish Colonial buildings for the 1935 California Pacific Exposition in Balboa Park. Buildings like Munk Laboratory are examples of Ruocco's strong rejection of historical styles in favor of a spare, modernist approach.

Munk Laboratory (aka the Institute of Geophysics and Planetary Physics) consists of two long low wings covered with vertical redwood siding and with deep redwood eaves and shade trellises. The wood is used ingeniously to create strong, simple geometric forms; the lines and grain of the wood also add a variety of patterns and textures. Like Wright's famous Fallingwater house in Pennsylvania, the Munk Laboratory is a strong work of architecture that responds organically to its site.

The south wing runs parallel to the nearby coastal bluff, set back beneath tall eucalyptus trees. The north wing runs perpendicular to the south wing. It ends near the edge of a cliff, perched precipitously above the ocean. Entry bridges connect the building to its sloped site. Walkways tunnel under the north building to surrounding locations.

A service yard tucked behind the building is barely visible from the road that climbs the hill between Munk and Revelle labs. Storage areas and workrooms line the service yard, with tall sliding doors of redwood and glass that make it easy to deliver laboratory equipment and supplies.

Ruocco and his wife, Ilse, an artist, were the glue that bonded a group of postwar San Diego modernists. The building is named for Scripps scientist Walter Munk. Munk and his wife, Judith, were part of the Ruoccos' salonlike group of friends and creative collaborators. Judith Munk was an artist and designer who collaborated with Ruocco on this building, as well as on the International Center building on the main UCSD campus.

9. Hydraulics Laboratory

Frank L. Hope, 1964

Sweeping up and over, the roof of the wood-and-glass Hydraulics Lab captures the form of a breaking ocean wave. It's a suitable image for a lab where research explores the properties of ocean waves as well as other ocean-related fluid

Hydraulics Laboratory

dynamics. Frank L. Hope is known for large buildings like banks, offices, and UCSD's Mandler and McGill Halls, but this building shows a gentler, organic side and illustrates his sensitivity to the natural beauty of this coastal hillside.

10. Revelle Laboratory for Geophysics
Liebhardt Weston Botton Architects, 1993

When Munk Laboratory outgrew its original building, architect Fred Liebhardt designed this empathetic expansion across the street. It is entirely in keeping with Ruocco's site-hugging, straightforward redwood building—not surprising since early in his career, Liebhardt worked for Ruocco.

Revelle Laboratory is a large building that could have overwhelmed the natural context, but thanks to its design, it's an unimposing structure that merges into its green surroundings. Spaces are allocated among four long, low redwood-and-glass buildings that step down the hilly site, connected by towers, bridges, decks, and outdoor walkways. The rustic forms give the impression of a group of garden pavilions. Exposed redwood-beam ends, redwood decks and railings, and red-framed circulation towers add a Japanese flavor.

Frank Lloyd Wright's influence is apparent at UCSD. Several architects who designed buildings at UCSD, including Robert Mosher and Fred Liebhardt, were mentored directly by Wright. The master's influence is apparent in the use of daringly cantilevered concrete forms, and in wood-and-glass buildings at Scripps and on the main campus. These latter buildings—mostly from the sixties and early seventies—flow with the natural terrain and use outdoor spaces to bring buildings and landscapes together.

Roger Revelle was one of the most important figures in the history of UCSD. As director of Scripps Institution in the fifties, he was a leader in the drive to build a

Roger and Ellen Revelle Laboratory for Geophysics

new University of California campus in La Jolla. Revelle's broad interest in sciences and liberal arts and his endless open-minded quest for fresh ideas resonate through legions of cutting-edge projects at the university today. The building named in his honor is the perfect representation of Revelle's logical and liberating ideas.

11. Scripps Institution of Oceanography Library
Liebhardt Weston and Goldman, 1975

Designing a library poses unusual challenges: How does one create a building that is architecturally exciting, pleasant to experience, and perhaps most importantly, a safe and secure place for thousands of books?

Eckart Library (named for Scripps scientist Carl H. Eckart) is the most provocative building at Scripps Institution, a sculptural concrete-and-glass complex of slanting, slotted roofs that admit gentle daylight and protect books from harsh direct sun. The building hugs a hillside south of Revelle Laboratory. Board-formed concrete walls bear the vertical grain of two-by-fours, which adds a handcrafted touch. Pebbly concrete used for slanted roofs provides a contrasting texture.

The approach to the main entrance is from the southwest: low, curved concrete walls lead under deep shading eaves to glass entry doors and a wall of glass.

Carl H. Eckart Library

Outdoor stairs around the building provide access for surfers, scientists, and visitors trekking down the hill.

12. Hubbs Hall
Liebhardt Weston Forester, 1976

Russell Forester designed the first Jack in the Box drive-in restaurant, a simple collection of cubes. As an artist, Forester painted spare, geometric shapes in the spirit of artists Piet Mondrian and Mark Rothko. Hubbs Hall displays the basic rectilinear forms favored by Forester and his partners, Fred Liebhardt and Eugene Weston.

Whereas nearby wood buildings recede into their sites and landscapes, Hubbs Hall is a forceful design. It utilizes bold, crisp forms that contrast sharply with a scrubby, coastal site. Four stories are defined by long horizontal lines of concrete between long rows of windows. Balconies overlook broad ocean views, shaded on the south by overhanging roofs and the balconies that project above them.

Research in this lab, known as the Marine Biology Research Division, covers many fields of marine biology, from identifying traits of fish species to genetic analysis of marine life such as abalone, sea urchins, and sharks. Hubbs also houses an experimental aquarium utilized for research by scientists from the Center for Marine Biodiversity and Conservation and the Center for Marine Genomics.

Bold, hard-edged forms present Hubbs Lab as a place of solid science and innovation, where research results in breakthroughs that will have a significant positive impact on the planet.

TOP: *Carl L. Hubbs Hall*
BOTTOM: *Ritter Hall*

13. Ritter Hall
Louis J. Gill, 1931

But for its red tile roof, Ritter Hall could be a building designed by Louis Gill's famous uncle, Irving Gill. Located just across the street from the elder Gill's Old Scripps Building, Ritter Hall consists of Louis Gill's original 1931 three-story building, plus a four-story structure that was added in 1956. Both the old and new buildings show the influence of Irving Gill. They feature smooth walls of concrete with no extraneous forms or decorative details.

Irving Gill is San Diego's greatest claim to fame in the history of twentieth-century architecture. In the first years of the twentieth century, he pioneered a style of plain white buildings inspired by California's simple white missions. Louis Gill was Irving's partner from 1914 to 1919 before he opened his own office. Once Irving Gill found his mature style of unadorned white boxes, he stayed with it for the remainder of his career. Louis was a more flexible architect whose designs are more varied.

Ritter Hall is named for William Ritter, the first director of Scripps Institution of Oceanography (from 1903 to 1923). The building contains labs, offices, conference rooms, and study rooms, and is used for research projects ranging from the study of assorted marine biology to global warming.

Gill's original structure lines the edge of Pawka Green, the landscaped plaza at the center of the Scripps campus. The second wing runs parallel to the Vaughan Hall laboratory building (1999), which replaced two other wings of Ritter Hall. A wide, landscaped pedestrian walkway runs between the buildings. Square windows run in orderly rows along the exterior of both buildings, recessed in the concrete so that shadow lines add texture to the exterior.

While Ritter Hall is basically a modernist box, the inclusion of the red clay tile roof (actually, it is only a decorative strip around the top of the building) gives it a hint of the Spanish Colonial style used by Louis Gill for other San Diego designs. His career covered an array of projects, from the first structures at the San Diego Zoo (including animal cages and grottos) to the County Administration Building in downtown San

Steven Sitter Pawka Memorial Green

Diego, where he directed a team of prominent San Diego architects also including Richard Requa, William Templeton Johnson, and Sam Hamill.

14. Pawka Green
Wallace Roberts & Todd, 2001

The evolution of planning at UCSD brought a commitment to the essential role of landscape architects in designing public spaces that unify the campus. Pawka Green was added at the center of the Scripps Institution of Oceanography campus to create a shared public space that brings the neighborhood together. Pawka Green is a landscaped public plaza with intimate seating areas and a small amphitheater that provides a great escape for scientists and an inviting place for visitors on their way to or from the beach.

Pawka Green fills an acre of open space surrounded by a veritable history of modern architecture. From the plaza, one can see nearly a hundred years' worth of modern architecture: Irving Gill's Old Scripps Building; Louis Gill's Ritter Hall; the contemporary Vaughan Hall designed by Hardy Holzman Pfeiffer; Risley and Gould's space-age Sumner Auditorium, blue-tiled Sverdrup Hall, and rustic wood New Director's office; and the angular wood-and-glass Robert Paine Scripps Forum by Safdie Rabines Architects.

Wallace Roberts & Todd set a new standard of drought-tolerant landscape design, proving that the approach can be both lush and water-conserving. While a few areas on the Scripps campus utilize grass, Pawka Green uses grass only as an accent material in a landscape that combines low maintenance hardscape (such as concrete and decomposed granite gravel) with low-water-use plants ranging from native Torrey pines to coral trees, aloe plants, and white Matilija poppies.

Low concrete walls define pocket gardens and seating areas. The walls are divided in sections that soften their visual impact, and geometric patterns add scale to large expanses of concrete. At the plaza's west edge, long, curved concrete benches define an amphitheater ideal for informal speeches and sunset performances.

Steven Sitter Pawka Memorial Green was endowed by Edward and Nancy Pawka in memory of their son Steven, who died of cancer in 1982. He completed his doctorate degree at Scripps in 1982.

15. Old Director's House
Julia Morgan, 1913

Old Director's House

Although Scripps Institution of Oceanography is now a major research center, during its humble beginnings Scripps looked more like a summer beach cottage resort than a scientific enterprise. It was known among scientists and locals as "the colony" and took its cues from the old Scripps beach cottages at La Jolla Cove. E. W. Scripps believed that "high thinking and modest living is to be the rule," and he built this house as well as several smaller bungalows to be used by researchers and academics. (At the time, the rent was $12 per month—if you could rent one of these cottages today, it would cost several hundred dollars per day.)

The Old Director's House is an excellent example of California Craftsman architecture, and the only San Diego building designed by Bay Area architect Julia Morgan, best known for her design of Hearst Castle in San Simeon along California's central coast. When Julia Morgan designed this place, Scripps had just built a road connecting the village of La Jolla to the new Scripps campus. The Old Scripps Building by Irving Gill was the only other major structure on the site. Scripps Pier, completed in 1916, had not yet been built.

William Ritter and his wife, Mary, were friends with Morgan and asked her to design the house, and the architect provided blueprints. They hired carpenter John Morgan to build it.

"We don't know if she gave him Julia Morgan's blueprints, but the Director's House bears a certain resemblance to those blueprints and incorporates details you can see today in some of Julia Morgan's houses in Berkeley that were built for the Ritter's friends," states Scripps archivist Deborah Day.[10] Those details include the front porch, stone garden walls, wood windows, hardwood floors, and built-in cabinets. It sits on a sloped site defined by a wall of smooth stones—stone walls such as this one are a hallmark of the California Craftsman style as practiced early in the twentieth century in San Diego and especially in Pasadena, where Greene and Greene's Gamble House is a world-famous landmark. (The Craftsman style takes its name from the fine craftsmanship applied to every detail by architects and builders.)

The Old Director's House is a two-story redwood bungalow with a brick chimney. It has a separate carriage house/garage with big sliding wood doors, from a time when car ownership was just becoming commonplace. The house features custom redwood front doors with vertical glass panels, wood windows, and patinated copper exterior lights. The garden is in the spirit of the Craftsman era in San Diego, with palm trees, various California native plants, a small lawn, and red geraniums lining the entry walk.

Even though Scripps Institution is now known around the world for its innovative research and has added several buildings, the spirit of the place, conveyed by lush landscaping and buildings constructed of basic materials such as concrete, wood, and stone, remains true to E. W. Scripps's original values.

16. Vaughan Hall

Ehrlich Rominger, Executive Architect/Hardy Holzman Pfeiffer, Design Architect, 1999

Like a canyon, a tall, tapered space between this building's two main sections is a defining feature that also brings daylight to a central courtyard. The four-story concrete and gray stucco building follows the contours of an access road to the north and a pedestrian walkway to the west that runs between Vaughan Hall and Ritter Hall. A slanted translucent awning atop a steel frame shades courtyard, while awnings protect teak windows (teak is an oily wood that withstands sunlight and moisture).

Shaded exterior windows and the central courtyard bring soft natural light to offices and labs, and the building also gets fresh air from windows that tilt out—natural ventilation is rare on structures this large in an era when most institutional buildings rely on mechanical heating, ventilating, and cooling.

Thomas Wayland Vaughan Hall

Outdoor stairs are emphasized as elegant sculptural features. They are designed with round slabs of concrete cantilevered from a central stalk, and with curved stainless-steel railings.

The landscape of evergreen and deciduous trees, and drought-tolerant shrubs and ground cover, closely follows the exterior's lines and angles to make a seamless merger of structure and site. Concrete benches create pocket gardens at the building's southwest corner, connecting it with the landscaped plaza at the core of the Scripps Institution of Oceanography campus.

Thomas Wayland Vaughan, the building's namesake, became Scripps's second director in 1923. He served until 1936, and his interests ranged from the growth rates of corals to the Cenozoic stratigraphy of the Caribbean. In a speech Vaughan gave in 1951 at the dedication of Scripps's new T. Wayland Vaughan Aquarium Museum (torn down years ago), he said that his goal as director was to expand the institution's mission to encompass physical, chemical, biological, and geological oceanography.[11] Vaughan had a hand in selecting his successor, Harald Sverdrup, and in a sense, these two innovators are together in perpetuity—Sverdrup Hall is only a few yards south of Vaughan's building.

Sumner Auditorium (Argo Hall)

17. Sumner Auditorium
Risley and Gould, 1960

Southern California architecture in the years following World War II was marked by a proliferation of experimental approaches. Los Angeles had Wallace Neff's dome houses and Frank Lloyd Wright's concrete block homes. In San Diego, led by Lloyd Ruocco, the quest was on for affordable, modern homes with open floors plans and simple structures with frames of steel or wood and walls of glass.

At Scripps Institution of Oceanography, Los Angeles architects Risley and Gould produced Sumner Auditorium, a rare gem of curved concrete with a surface pattern of narrow vertical grooves. The auditorium has the same DNA as boomerang coffee tables, kidney-shaped pools, and space-age designs such as the 1961 Theme Building at Los Angeles International Airport, a podlike building elevated on spidery-thin concrete legs.

The auditorium's sweeping curve is an example of unified function and form. Situated at the opposite end of an open pedestrian arcade from Sverdrup Hall, the auditorium's curve is a subtle means of crowd control that invites visitors to queue up along the wall and follow the curve to the entrance. Positioned between the hard-edged verticals and horizontals of Sverdrup Hall to the south and the kinetic diagonals and bold materials of Vaughan Hall to the north, Sumner Auditorium's sweeping off-white wall is a gentle counterpoint that ties the neighborhood together.

Sumner Auditorium is named for Francis Bertody Sumner, a marine biologist who joined the Scripps faculty in 1913 and stayed until his death in 1945. Prior to Scripps, he directed the U.S. Bureau of Fisheries Laboratory in Woods Hole, Massachusetts, and served as a naturalist on the research vessel *Albatross*, an iron-hulled steamer launched in 1882 and believed by many to be the first ship specifically built for marine research. Sumner went aboard in 1910 to conduct a biological survey of San Francisco Bay. Sumner's first research project at Scripps was a twelve-year study of beach mice (Peromyscus). He brought species from diverse geographic locations to Scripps and observed how their colors changed when they all occupied the same habitat. This work led to Sumner's studies of the coloration of fish according to underwater habitat.

Sumner believed in science as an ongoing quest to understand our world—research might not yield immediate answers or marketable products, but the search for new information must continue. In light of his adventuresome spirit and frequent research voyages, the curved "prow" of Sumner Auditorium pays fitting tribute to the scientist.

18. Sverdrup Hall
Risley and Gould, 1960

California's tradition of the application of colorful tiles in architecture dates back to the early twentieth-century Craftsman style as well as the Mediterranean Revival of the twenties and thirties. Chromatic tiles can be found around pools and in bathrooms and kitchens, while earth tones are more common for fireplaces. Risley and Gould made unusual use of tiles in the design of Sverdrup Hall. The building's exterior, which is made of tiny aquamarine tiles, makes an oceanic impression from a

Sverdrup Hall

distance. Up close, the fine tile-and-grout work transports the visitor to a time when even a modern building such as this one could have had a handcrafted exterior.

Sverdrup Hall is a long flat-roofed three-story rectangular building that frames the sound end of Pawka Green, the big open space in the middle of the Scripps Institution of Oceanography campus. The building runs east-west, with the long sides facing north and south. The exterior consists of a concrete frame with the tiled exterior walls recessed within the frame. Rows of square windows emphasize the building's long, low profile.

One entrance is on the west end, with double glass doors beneath a two-story wall of windows that floods the lobby with daylight. Smaller entrances can be found on other sides of the building. On the south side, a sidewalk leads to a footbridge over a dry creek bed. On the north, broad steps descend to Pawka Green between Sverdrup Hall and Sumner Auditorium.

Norwegian oceanographer and meteorologist Harald Ulrik Sverdrup served as the third director of Scripps, from 1936 to 1948. When he arrived, he was disappointed to discover that much of the work taking place in Scripps labs focused on scientific research unrelated to the ocean.[12] Sverdrup realized that the Pacific Ocean represented a vast, unexplored treasure trove of research data waiting to be discovered. He set out to put the ocean in oceanography, and his first research voyage investigated ocean conditions during the sardine-spawning season (his findings would later help California's sardine-fishing industry). In 1939, Sverdrup began work on a definitive oceanography textbook. Coauthored with fellow Scripps scientist Martin W. Johnson and Ronald H. Fleming, *The Oceans: Their Physics, Chemistry and General Biology* was published in 1942. During his twelve years at Scripps, Sverdrup also collaborated with Scripps scientist Walter Munk to produce sea, surf, and ocean swell forecasts for Allied landings in North Africa, Europe, and the Pacific during World War II. He also developed the first accurate scientific description of ocean circulation, known as the Sverdrup balance.

Old Scripps Building

19. Old Scripps Building
Irving Gill, 1910

Architect Irving Gill was at the peak of his career when Ellen Browning Scripps hired him to design the first building at what would become Scripps Institution of Oceanography. The first seaside marine lab in the United States opened in 1871 in Woods Hole, Massachusetts. Gill's George H. Scripps Memorial Marine Biological Laboratory gave California and the West Coast an oceanfront lab of its own, extending the modern idea of conducting intensive ocean research right next to the ocean. Over the years, the Old Scripps Building has been used as a working laboratory, a public aquarium, a classroom, and an office for Scripps's directors.

Gill had spent time in the early 1890s working alongside Frank Lloyd Wright in the Chicago office of architect Louis Sullivan. Gill arrived in San Diego in 1893, and after a decade of designing houses in the Craftsman/Prairie style, he began to explore a minimalist modern approach that became his signature.

Gill was a pioneer in concrete construction. His La Jolla Women's Club is a masterpiece of flat walls, arches, trellises, and courtyards, built with tilt-up concrete walls, a process in which concrete is poured in forms on the ground and tilted up into place. For the Scripps building, the walls were poured in vertical forms to create a simple rectangular laboratory on a bluff only yards from the ocean. Gill adopted the Kahn system (named for Moritz Kahn, the early twentieth-century engineer who invented it) of steel-reinforcing bars lined with small spikes that gain a hold in the concrete, with the bars connected to each other by small steel crosspieces. Concrete utilizing the Kahn steel system was much stronger when subjected to stress from several directions, as in an earthquake.

Like other Gill buildings from this era, the Scripps lab is unornamented. It is a rectangular, flat-roofed, two-story box, lined with two rows of evenly spaced windows, and with a small balcony that pops out on the second level above the entry. Large windows maximize natural light inside the labs, as requested by William Ritter, the institution's first director. Gill was known for interior innovation, and the building includes skylights and glass-block floor sections that bring daylight to labs and other rooms.

When Ritter arrived at Scripps to be its first director, he and his wife lived on the second floor of the Old Scripps Building for three years until a director's house was built. Conveniently, he could get up in the morning and go downstairs to work in the labs. The second floor also included the lab's only classroom and, until 1950, the director's office.

Although gardens are important features of most Gill buildings, the Old Scripps Building had no landscape plan to speak of other than a few shrubs. Considering the time and the context of its design and construction, this is not surprising. Photos of La Jolla circa 1910 show a virtually vacant expanse of scrubby land along the Pacific Ocean. Today, Gill's building sits at the edge of a landscaped central plaza; at the turn of the century, the same site lay along a rocky coastal bluff. It now houses the offices of the graduate program.

Gill's career fell off in the years after 1915, when the Panama-California Exposition in San Diego's Balboa Park sparked a fascination with Mediterranean Revival architecture that continues today. When Gill died in 1936 in Oceanside, about twenty-five miles up the coast from San Diego, his death certificate listed his occupation as "laborer." Over the years, many of his finest buildings were razed, as modernism's simple, logical virtues went unappreciated. Like other lucky Gill buildings that survived, this one is listed on the National Register of Historical Places and, short of an unexpected apocalypse, will stand for decades to come.

20. New Director's Office
Risley and Gould, 1959

Architects Risley and Gould designed several multistory concrete buildings on the main UCSD campus, but the New Director's Office is a direct descendant of the small beach cottages on which the architects built their reputation. The one-story U-shaped building (plus basement) wraps three sides of Irving Gill's Old Scripps Building, only yards from the ocean.

Exterior walls are board-and-batten—wide vertical pine boards with narrow vertical battens covering the seams—a method of construction seen often in California beach houses from the fifties and sixties. Pairs of roof beams project beyond walls to support the overhanging flat roof. Large square windows run the full length of the building's west side, where the concrete floor slab extends outside as an ocean-view balcony with a steel-cable railing.

New Director's Office

The building contains forty-five small offices, a conference room, and a kitchen. The entrance is on the building's south side, accessed from a walkway going past a rose garden. The landscape surrounding the house also includes palm trees, agapanthuses, and rose vines that climb wood trellises on the exterior walls.

Newer buildings have transformed the center of the Scripps campus into a place that is probably denser, bigger, and busier than the institution's founders ever imagined. By maintaining smaller, older Scripps buildings such as this one, UCSD preserves the essential light, open, sun- and sea-worshipping spirit that dates back to the early years and continues to rejuvenate researchers today.

21. Scripps Seaside Forum
Safdie Rabines Architects, 2009

Designed by Safdie Rabines Architects, this new conference center overlooks La Jolla Shores Beach and Scripps Pier, and is a short conch shell's throw from the sand. A cluster of curves, diagonals, and boxes, the complex takes its cues from the California vernacular of beach cottages, piers, and lifeguard towers, like the one just a few yards away on the beach.

The plan includes a two-story conference center with a first-floor auditorium and second-level terrace and rooftop restaurant, and a row of wood-and-glass cabanas for small meetings, angled for great views of the ocean and to maintain privacy for each room's patio. The 275-seat auditorium is tucked into the gently sloping site, minimizing its impact on ocean views from the Scripps campus, as well as views of Scripps from the beach below.

Buildings combine tan stucco, wood siding in narrow horizontal strips, and liberal expanses of glass. The building's roof slopes down like the face of a wave. Glass railings along the terraces preserve views while providing protection from ocean breezes that often buffet coastal buildings. Trellises of narrow wood strips shade the outdoor spaces, filtering daylight into a fine pattern of parallel light-and-shadow lines.

The back wall, facing away from the beach, curves along the edge of the parking lot like the bow of a ship and wraps the rooftop restaurant, providing wind protection.

TOP AND BOTTOM: *Robert Paine Scripps Seaside Forum for Science, Society, and the Environment*

Steps lead up from the parking lot to a walkway between two sections of the building. Along the walkway, walls are lined with furniture-grade horizontal wood siding, clear-sealed against the weather so that the rich grain is revealed. Beds that buffer the building's edges are planted with trees and small drought-tolerant plants in regular rows.

The building is named for Robert Paine Scripps, son of Scripps's founder E. W. Scripps and nephew of the institution's benefactor, Ellen Browning Scripps. After the senior Scripps passed away in 1926, his son assumed the responsibility for the family's ongoing support, increasing the annual contribution to help the institution survive the Depression.

On its oceanfront site, which is passed by thousands of beachgoers every week, the Robert Paine Scripps Forum combines a modest residential scale with exciting forms and outdoor spaces that make the most of the extraordinary views and temperate climate.

22. Scripps Pier
Ferver Engineering, 1988

San Diego has several piers, but Scripps Institution of Oceanography has the only one devoted to research. The original 1,000-foot wood-and-concrete pier was completed in 1916, but by the eighties had become a rickety, storm-battered safety risk. After Navy Seals demolished the original pier as a training exercise, it was replaced with a $3.95 million, 1,084-foot-long, 22.5-foot-wide reinforced concrete pier in 1988. (The 1,971-foot concrete pier in Ocean Beach is San Diego County's longest.)

Poised thirty-two feet above the mean low level sea elevation, the pier consists of precast, pre-stressed concrete slabs supported by thirty-seven concrete bents.[13] The slabs vary in thickness from eight inches at the longitudinal center to five inches at the edge. They are fixed at one end and have the capacity for shock-absorbing movement using a slide/bearing assembly consisting of stainless steel plates.

The bents consist of vertical piles connected by horizontal caps. The twenty-four-inch diameter octagonal piles are made of precast, prestressed concrete. They are set fifteen feet deep in the shale seabed, and they range in total height from thirty-eighth feet near the shore to seventy-eight feet at the end of the pier. The precast reinforced concrete caps are twenty-two and a half feet long.

For nearly one hundred years the pier has extended the reach of Scripps into coastal waters rich with sea life. Fresh seawater is piped from the pier to research labs and to the Stephen Birch Aquarium. Research boats launched from a hoist at the end of the pier, following in the wake of vessels lowered into the water from the original pier, including Jacques Cousteau's *Diving Saucer*.

Ellen Browning Scripps Memorial Pier

The sea surrounding the pier teems with plant and animal life. Two underwater canyons cut cross the ocean floor a few hundred yards offshore. Hundreds of feet deep, the canyons are beyond the range of recreational divers.

Scientists have analyzed data collected from the pier since 1916. Subjects of investigation range from plankton, ocean temperature, coastal air quality, the behavior of sound waves underwater, and seawater salinity, to the deep underwater canyons off La Jolla. In one study, researchers used air samples and data about wind speed and direction to determine what kinds of particles were in the air. They traced a trail of carbon emissions along the highway from San Diego to Las Vegas, among other patterns. Findings such as these have long-term implications for the health of people and the planet. The massive tsunami that hit Sumatra in 2004 was detected by equipment at Scripps Pier.

Pumps on the end of the pier provide 1.8 million gallons of fresh seawater each day to Scripps labs as well as tanks at the Birch Aquarium. A building at the end of the pier contains four labs and several storage rooms. On the roof is a weather station with a sensor-equipped boom that collects wind and temperature readings. Of course there is a webcam too: http://www.sccoos.org/data/piers/

The pier is a San Diego landmark. At night its lights are visible for miles up and down the coast. Locals make plans to meet "by the pier," generations of surfers have ridden waves in its shadow, and kayakers paddle (illegally) between its pilings. Countless photos have been taken of the pier, including one by famed photographer Ansel Adams, whose iconic black-and-white image from 1966 is titled, simply, "The Scripps Pier."

WALK TWO: THEATRE DISTRICT

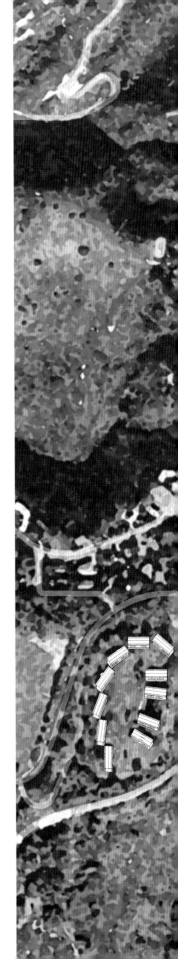

Mandell Weiss Center for Performing Arts: Mandell Weiss Theatre

1. Mandell Weiss Theatre
Tucker, Sadler and Associates, 1982

When the Mandell Weiss opened, the La Jolla Playhouse celebrated a rebirth after many years in the dark. Founded in 1947 by Gregory Peck, Dorothy McGuire, and Mel Ferrer, the playhouse originally performed in a high school auditorium. With La Jolla Playhouse as UCSD's resident company, the Department of Dance is able to offer internships. Another benefit of having the playhouse on campus is a ready supply of seasoned professionals who teach university classes.

In the new theater and under artistic director Des McAnuff, the company soon exceeded high expectations with a series of award-winning plays, many of them original works that ended up on Broadway. Dramas that became Broadway hits (many of them directed by McAnuff) include *The Who's Tommy*, *Thoroughly Modern Millie* (which also launched the career of actress Sutton Foster), *Big River*, *A Walk in the Woods*, and *Jersey Boys*. As of 2009, the company had won twenty-one Tony Awards.

The 492-seat proscenium-arch theater (the proscenium is the frame above the stage) has a large stage and sophisticated lighting. The structure consists of modest stucco forms tucked into a rolling landscape of lawn and trees. The tallest piece of the building, visible from La Jolla Village Drive, contains a fly space (for hanging scenery) that accommodates large productions. For elaborate musicals and other productions, the stage is technically equipped for moving sets that automatically appear and disappear during a performance.

The Weiss theater's entry court, lobby, and large roof deck provide places where the company can host receptions and special events for donors like the late Mandell

Weiss, who gave $1.3 million toward this building and $1.4 million more to help build the adjacent Mandell Weiss Forum theater. He was the playhouse's premiere patron until his death in 1994 at age 102.

2. Mandell Weiss Forum
Antoine Predock Architects, 1991

Where Predock's nearby Molli and Arthur Wagner Dance Theatre is of a pinkish stucco that captures a buoyant mood, the Mandell Weiss Forum's fathomless gray evokes shadows and mystery, a fitting metaphor for the drama of theater.

Like a good drama, the theater building forces playgoers to see themselves in new and novel ways. By the time they reach their seats to watch a play, they have been directed by the architect's design through a series of dramatic experiences.

From the parking lot, visitors pass through the eucalyptus grove, with its dappled light and fresh, distinctive fragrance. They emerge in a clearing in front of a 270-foot-long mirror wall, behind which the building is hidden. As they approach the wall, they become aware of their reflections; posture and stride change noticeably. Rustling leaves underfoot give way to the crunching sound of a gravel strip along the wall, a subliminal signal that the theater is near. At dusk, small lights flicker like stage footlights along the length of this median. Anticipation builds as visitors press together through an opening in the glass wall into a courtyard. To the right is famed chef Wolfgang Puck's contemporary Asian restaurant Jai, encased in a steel-and-glass building by Roto Architects. To the left, a switchback ramp leads up, then up again, to the second-level main entrance. The final scene in this drama comes when visitors descend into the theater to take their seats.

The 400-seat theater complements La Jolla Playhouse's other two venues. Seats are configured in a semicircle that slants down to the stage, putting the audience close to the performers and providing excellent views. Many of La Jolla Playhouse's new and experimental plays take place here, including dramas developed in the Page to Stage program, where audiences can observe the development of a new play from scratch—from script to readings, revisions, workshops, and rehearsals. Playwright Doug Wright's *I Am My Own Wife* was a Page to Stage project that premiered in New York City and won both a Pulitzer Prize and a Tony in 2004.

The Forum, along with the Wagner Theatre, defines the edges of the Theatre District. The Forum's mirror wall projects out toward the entrance road, like a billboard without words that says "drama." The dance thrusts its pink curved wall toward the access road behind the site, presenting another signal to visitors. The original Mandell Weiss Theatre was hidden within the eucalyptus grove. Now, UCSD has a cluster of buildings as attention-getting as the performances unfolding inside them.

Mandell Weiss Center for Performing Arts: Mandell Weiss Forum

3. Jacobs Center for La Jolla Playhouse
Roto Architects with FSY Architects, 2005

Swooping above the entrance, the center's curved roof is a jolt of energy that magnetizes the shapes behind it into a cohesive design. The jutting roof's playful shape gives a warm welcome to visitors, sheltering them as they close umbrellas, hunt for tickets, or take a final sip of coffee.

While the building uses basic materials, the craftsmanship is sophisticated. The curves and angles of the roof and brick wall over the box office added an extra challenge for construction crews. From a distance the brick wall's non-parallel horizontal lines create a sense of vibration or movement reminiscent of the movement of actors during a performance. A close look at the brick wall will reveal the difficulty of aligning bricks of countless sizes to create a precisely variegated texture.

This newest building in the Theatre District is also its most complex and provocative. Where Antoine Predock's Forum is a minimalist mystery, the Jacobs

Joan & Irwin Jacobs Center for La Jolla Playhouse

Center is a kinetic 3-D collage of cubes and angles rendered in steel, glass, wood, and masonry. Firing off sparks in several directions, the building has a primal power similar to the creative experiments that take place within.

The Jacobs Center's prime feature is the 450-seat Sheila and Hughes Potiker Theatre, a flexible "black box" that meets needs different than the Mandell Weiss Theatre with its large Broadway-style curtained proscenium stage or than the Forum, with its stage that juts into the audience.

Exposed roof beams outside and inside add natural accents to the concrete, steel, and glass. In the atrium lobby, railings and walls repeat the building's pattern of diagonal accents against strong horizontal and vertical forms.

Under an agreement between La Jolla Playhouse and UCSD's Department of Theatre and Dance, the two entities share resources. Theater graduate students take residencies at the Playhouse in acting, directing, design, and stage management. Undergrads serve as Playhouse interns. Playhouse staff members teach theater classes, and theater faculty may be employed by the Playhouse as directors, actors, and in other capacities. Artists who studied at UCSD and graduated to successful careers include actors James Avery, Yareli Arizmendi, Ricardo Antonio Chavira, and writer Rachel Axler, who became the first female writer on *The Daily Show*.

The black box is a more flexible space than either of its siblings; it can be configured for a variety of staging and seating arrangements. Colors for the black box and main rehearsal room are inspired by the site's natural colors. Inside the black box, an overhead steel grid provides infinite lighting options. Together with three rehearsal rooms, the Jacobs Center is a well-equipped "laboratory" where emerging playwrights, producers, directors, actors, and production people hone their craft. Vocal dynamics are an essential tool for actors, and refined acoustics help actors to give refined performances. Performance, rehearsal, and teaching spaces in this building are acoustically isolated from each other, yet each room is also very responsive to vocal variations.

Architect Michael Rotondi (his company's name, Roto, is derived from his name) has expressed that architecture incorporates elements of theater. Like the narrative structure of a play, a building creates a series of distinctive experiences. There are moments of joy and elation, as well as darker, mysterious moods. Rather than with words, an architect shapes reactions through materials, proportions, lighting, and the placement of walls, glass, and ceiling.

Of all of these, glass may be the most powerful. It can control what is visible and what is not. During the design process, Des McAnuff, then the Playhouse's artistic director, repeatedly emphasized his own fascination with the powers of glass and wanted the building to function like an open office, where transparency would foster an environment in which Playhouse staff—ranging from lighting designers to marketing and development types—could see each other and feed off the excitement of their shared mission. The results of the dialogue between Rotondi and McAnuff are apparent in the Jacobs theater, with its glass walls of various sizes and shapes, placed at strategic locations and at various angles.

Filling the gap between the dance studio building and the other two theaters, Jacobs Center defines the courtyard at the heart of the complex and provides experimental space where new plays, playwrights, and actors can develop. The placement and configuration of the new building in this central location unified UCSD's Theatre District into one of the most exciting neighborhoods on campus.

4. Wagner Dance Studio
Antoine Predock Architects, 1997

Trace a dancer's patterns across a hardwood floor and you'll find some of the curves and angles that define the Wagner Dance Studio. Architect Antoine Predock is inspired by the work of famed choreographer Merce Cunningham, who revolutionized modern dance by introducing spontaneous, nontraditional dance movements. Predock conceives of buildings as a means of choreographing a visitor's experience by creating a series of dramatic spaces.

The architect also takes inspiration from regional contexts. Here, as in other projects throughout the American Southwest, he uses smooth stucco walls with deep-set window openings, with an effect reminiscent of California's missions and early adobe ranch houses.

From Scholar's Drive South, the campus road leading past the building, a freestanding stucco wall sweeps into a eucalyptus grove with the primal impact of an authentic mission wall. The trees cast lacy shadow patterns on the wall, and the wall is pierced by openings that offer glimpses of dancers in the studios. Farther into the grove, the stucco wall becomes a wall of glass that continues the curve to the building's entry courtyard, with its "landscape" of fallen eucalyptus leaves. Dance studios are enclosed by tall windows that provide dancers with views of the trees and the changing patterns of daylight and shadows. Studios feature dark ceilings and mirrored walls that place the dancers in a state of limbo where they can rehearse undistracted by the thrum of campus life. Dancing here is like waltzing in a magical forest.

In a career that began in the seventies, Predock has explored modern variations on the simple buildings of early California and New Mexico. With their unconventional, graceful shapes, and surprising collages of material, light, and shadow, Predock's buildings seem to capture an energy common to the two places, which are both known for their ongoing fascination with mysticism and spirituality.

Predock refers to architecture as a "a physical ride, an experience of moving through three-dimensional spaces defined by buildings and landscapes."[1] He sees his architecture as elemental, rooted in air, earth, fire, and water. Trained as a landscape architect, Predock thinks of architecture and landscape as inseparable. Indeed, his dance building recedes into the eucalyptus grove to create an ideal merger of structure and nature.

Wagner Dance Studio

WALK THREE: REVELLE COLLEGE

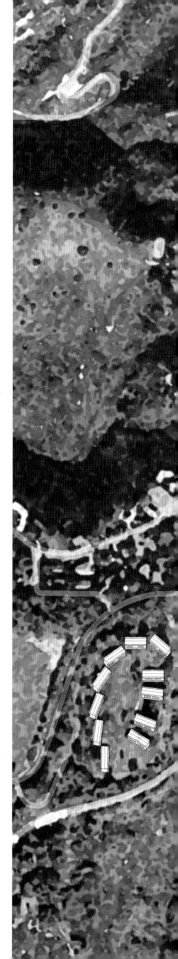

1. Revelle Student Housing: Atlantis, Meteor, Beagle, Challenger, Discovery, Galathea
Robert Alexander, 1965

"The Fleets" are an armada of six residential buildings, each housing eighty students, with landscaped courtyards that bring the neighborhood together. Famed Scripps oceanographer Roger Revelle took a leading role in founding UCSD, and Revelle College had close ties with Scripps Institution of Oceanography, so it is fitting that these buildings are named after famous ships. *Discovery* and *Challenger*, for instance, were Scripps research vessels, and *Beagle* was the boat that carried Charles Darwin to the Galapagos Islands.

TOP: *Revelle Student Housing*
BOTTOM: *Argo Hall, Blake Hall*

Architect Robert Alexander's original 1963 campus master plan outlined an architectural identity for each college. Alexander's student housing reinforces the spare, modernist style of Revelle College. These four-story sandstone buildings mimic the color and texture of coastal sandstone bluffs. The beach metaphor extends to nearby sand volleyball courts.

Despite their simplicity, the Fleets are full of spirit. V-shaped roofs resemble soaring birds. Projecting walls and floor slabs provide privacy and shade—simple design solutions serving practical needs without extraneous elements. Pine and liquidambar trees change with the seasons.

Before drafting UCSD's early master plan and designing buildings on campus, Alexander worked for architect Richard Neutra. The famed modernist was known for a humanistic approach—although austere and hard-edged, his buildings responded to the practical and emotional needs of their users. Alexander's modernist student housing has details that make the complex comfortable and inviting while creating a sense of community. The friendly relationships of buildings to each other and to the outdoors and the careful planning of courtyards between buildings create an intimate neighborhood within a large campus.

2. Argo Hall and Blake Hall
Tucker, Sadler and Bennett, 1967

Courtyards in California date back to the chain of missions built by the Franciscans during the eighteenth and nineteenth centuries in their efforts to spread Christianity among Native Americans. These long, low buildings were configured in L or U shapes around a central courtyard. Later, the courtyard plan was adapted for adobe ranch houses, apartments, motels, and modern houses, arranged, like the missions, around a courtyard. Within these student dormitories, the courtyards create a shared commons and assure that each room gets daylight and fresh air.

Argo and Blake halls flank a landscaped pedestrian walk that heads west from Revelle Plaza. Argo houses 350 students, Blake 150 with spaces for offices, a lounge, and a computer lab on the first floor, as well as a second lounge, kitchen, patio, and redwood sundecks on the fourth. Open breezeways at their bases connect these buildings with campus walkways. Outdoor stairs provide access to the upper levels (also served by elevators).

The experience of moving through the buildings outdoors contrasts with indoor circulation at Muir College's Tioga and Tenaya residential towers.

Argo and Blake incorporate concrete box-frame construction consisting of horizontal floor slabs and vertical walls. They are both elevated atop ground-floor pedestals that give them a floating appearance. Similar to many other UCSD buildings of their era, both feature narrow vertical fins and windows, which add interesting texture and serve the practical purpose of providing both daylight and privacy.

Architect Hal Sadler, like many other UCSD architects, is a product of fifties California modernism. He earned his architecture degree at the University of Southern California and landed his first job in the Los Angeles office of architect A. Quincy Jones, the designer of UCSD's Mandeville Center. After Sadler moved to San Diego and opened an office of his own with partners, he became a highly regarded designer of houses as well as large-scale projects, including the downtown Union Bank building. At UCSD, Sadler, with his modest designs, deferred to the scale and approximate style of nearby campus buildings designed by peers (and friends) such as Robert Mosher, Ward Deems, and Fred Liebhardt.

3. Natural Sciences Building
Bohlin Cywinski Jackson with Bundy/Thompson, 2004

Built on the sciences, Revelle College recruited leading researchers from around the country and grew rapidly in size and reputation. From the beginning the high quality of the campus's planning and architecture were part of the attraction. As programs expanded and new technologies emerged, existing buildings were updated and new

Natural Sciences Building

buildings were added. Today, UCSD is considered one of the world's top institutions for scientific research. In 2008, for instance, UCSD chemist Roger Tsien was awarded the Nobel Prize for research that utilized a green fluorescent protein from jellyfish as a medium for observing previously invisible processes such as the movement of proteins from one part of a cell to another. Tsien's breakthrough opened a path that could lead to new cures for a variety of diseases.

The six-story structure brings together biochemistry, molecular biology, and biophysics in one building to encourage collaborative research. The building's design points the way toward a future campus that is animated, urban, and innovative.

Situated at the western edge of campus, the L-shaped concrete building is highly visible near the busy intersection of Torrey Pines Road and La Jolla Shores Drive. Bold concrete forms, banks of windows shaded by steel mesh screens, and open stair towers make a well-proportioned 3-D sculpture.

The building's main entrance is on the east, next to Ridge Walk, the north/south pedestrian promenade through the campus situated along what was old Highway 101. Close to the entrance sits a grove of jacaranda trees in a bed of decomposed granite, a garden configuration inspired by early California mission gardens. Nearby, a rolling lawn leads to a glade of mature evergreen trees as old as the campus itself. Through the entry doors is the two-story lobby atrium, where the curvy edge of a mezzanine snakes through the space. Many offices, conference rooms, and balconies have ocean views, and transparent glass at the ground floor adds additional glimpses of the landscape.

The building is also full of rich surfaces: precast concrete panels, angled concrete buttresses, and a two-story wall of glass that brings daylight to the atrium.

If possible, this building should be visited just before dusk, when the deepening blue sky, orange horizon, and long shadows make this California beauty very ready for her close-up.

4. Pacific Hall

Mitchell Giurgola Architects and Austin/Hansen/Fehlman, 1994

Sky blue awnings line the curve of the building's west end, greeting motorists like blinking eyelashes. Pacific Hall and the Natural Sciences Building next door offer visitors strong images of UCSD's emerging urban character. The planning of campus expansion during the building boom of the nineties and into the subsequent decade became increasingly complex. Planners have gone to great lengths to assure that new buildings work well with both the existing campus and surrounding off-campus neighborhoods.

This building, for example, presents a sleek stone wall to the street—an attractive design gesture to motorists. On the campus side, however, it drops from six stories to four with an open white pavilion that tells pedestrians how to get inside. Details give the building its charm: A stair tower connects six-story and four-story sections. The service entry and loading dock are tucked out of sight on the building's northwest corner. The north side of the building is designed to capture gentle, indirect north light. The south side features deep-set windows and the blue awnings to prevent direct sunlight from overheating the interiors.

Pacific Hall is home to an array of research in chemistry and biochemistry, including nanotechnology, the photophysics of nanophase materials, medical applications of nanotube materials, and thermal response of porous Si-based vapor sensors. Specialty areas here include the Small Molecule X-Ray Facility.

In the early years, the sciences at UCSD operated out of stone-and-concrete buildings that sustained the misperception of science as a precise but a not very cheery enterprise. Newer buildings like Pacific Hall reveal the truth: science is as

colorful and exciting as the arts. Increasingly, artists and scientists collaborate at UCSD. Buildings like Pacific Hall convey the message that the scientific research taking place inside is as visceral as a concert of experimental music or a play by Samuel Beckett—and that whether a building is designed for the sciences or the arts, it deserves innovative, intriguing architecture.

Pacific Hall

5. Bonner Hall
Risley, Gould & Van Heuklyn, 1964

David Mahlon Bonner Hall looks much the same as it did when it opened, and it's one of the quirkier examples of modernism on campus. Its use has changed with evolving technology. Today, it houses a cryoelectron microscopy lab and the Center for Molecular Genetics. Research includes cancer, viral infections, and autoimmune diseases.

Risley, Gould & Van Heuklyn's design incorporates the box-frame system pioneered in the fifties by Danish structural engineer Ove Arup (whose company engineered various UCSD buildings, though not this one). The box-frame system combines concrete slabs and walls into a rigid, efficient structural frame that affords uncluttered interior spaces.

Bonner Hall

Here, the floor slabs project beyond the ends of the building to become outdoor decks and outdoor hallways connected by diagonal stairs. This open circulation plan takes advantage of San Diego's great weather and provides a smooth transition from the building to the adjacent courtyard between Bonner and Mayer Halls.

Bonner Hall reflects the sixties fascination with precast concrete panels incorporating colorful stone and tile. In 1966, to promote the use of concrete, the Portland Cement Association published the book *Exploring Color and Texture* to showcase dozens of examples of precast concrete panels, columns, and trusses. (The book is available as a free download at www.concrete.org/bookstore.) The colored stones and earth-toned tiles incorporated in the surfaces of the exterior wall panels help pick up colors from surrounding eucalyptus trees.

Before he opened his own practice, architect Winchley Risley worked for Bertram Goodhue and Carleton Winslow, who designed some of San Diego's best-known buildings, including several for the 1915 Panama-California Exposition in Balboa Park (they remain today). While Risley's own work did not incorporate the decorative details of Goodhue and Winslow's Spanish Revival and Art Deco styles, it is obvious that he learned some lessons about creating dramatic spaces like the plazas, arcades, and courtyards throughout Balboa Park.

Bonner Hall is named after David Bonner, who was recruited from Yale University to join the UCSD faculty and serve as founding chairman of the Department of Biology when the new university opened in 1964. (Bonner was also instrumental in launching UCSD's medical school.) Bonner suffered from Hodgkin's lymphoma, which helps explain his interest in genetics. The building's commemorative bronze plaque reads: "[Bonner] showed the way toward new horizons in biology and medicine."

Maria Goeppert and Joseph Edward Mayer Hall

6. Mayer Hall
Risley and Gould, 1963

Mayer Hall Addition
MBT Architecture, 2008

Physics was a founding science at UCSD, and university leaders recruited world-renowned faculty, including Maria Goeppert-Mayer. The structural design of buildings and the impact of earthquakes are subjects of research at UCSD, and Mayer Hall presents a case study in the evolution of earthquake-resistant engineering.

The building combines sixties concrete construction with structural reinforcement and new features added during a 2008 renovation and addition, including a glass stair tower that serves as a visible icon along Ridge Walk, the main pedestrian path through Revelle College. The renovation also upgraded Mayer Hall's research labs.

Mayer Hall was built with poured-in-place concrete slabs and walls. On the outside, it has the same pebbled concrete panels as Bonner Hall. Like Bonner, it also features deep balconies that serve as outdoor corridors, giving the building an open, inviting appeal.

But its most dramatic detail—and one of the most spectacular architectural elements on campus—is the three-story bridge between Mayer Hall and Bonner Hall. Flared precast concrete columns are stacked on three levels to create an organic pattern reminiscent of the columns Frank Lloyd Wright used in his thirties design for the Johnson Wax Headquarters in Wisconsin.

Mayer Hall is named after Maria Goeppert-Mayer, who was awarded the Nobel Prize in Physics in 1963 for her work in nuclear physics. The Mayer name figures prominently in UCSD's history, and her husband, Joseph Mayer, was a chemical physicist whose early work included research in atomic weapons. Both had been among a circle of scientists involved with developing the atomic bomb, including eventual UCSD faculty member Harold Urey as well as Edward Teller, the "father of the hydrogen bomb." The couple joined UCSD's faculty in 1960.

Physics has played a catalytic role in UCSD's growth since the formative years of the late fifties. The university was launched during a Cold War boom in sciences and technology. A significant number of early faculty members were physicists, and the discipline has remained at the core of UCSD's science curriculum. By the late nineties, the department was rapidly outgrowing its buildings on campus.

Easing the space crunch resulting from 15,000 students enrolled in biophysics, plasma physics, astrophysics, and other specialty areas, this triangular five-story addition more than doubles Mayer Hall's size. The 45,000-square-foot addition includes offices and state-of-the art labs, and its design responds to the site and the scale and appearance of surrounding buildings. A new landscaped courtyard connects this building with the original Mayer Hall and Bonner Hall, just to the north.

The addition is situated down a slope behind the original building and sheltered by mature eucalyptus. The exterior is skinned with translucent and transparent glass, metal, and textured concrete. These materials are used in various combinations depending on the building's exposure to sunlight and the need to provide shade for interior spaces.

The addition's structural core is a system of poured-in-place concrete columns and beams matching the structural system of the original building. Inside, the building is a wonder of unusual forms, natural light, and interesting finishes. On each level, two hallways outline long sides of a triangle. Each hallway is lined with windows that provide views and daylight. Yellow walls alternate with concrete

Bridge between Bonner and Mayer Halls

surfaces; floors are covered with off-white, yellow, and green linoleum. Even small details are unique, such as the Deco-style hallway lights and elegant wood doors. New labs are appointed with the latest equipment and some of them have windows (not common in older buildings). Offices, meeting rooms, and reception areas are all similarly inviting.

Since its opening, Mayer Hall has become known as one of the coolest buildings on this part of campus—an unusual and inventive combination of old and new. It is a place where one can often find prospective faculty and grad students taking a tour that may clinch their decision to come to UCSD.

7. Urey Hall

Risley and Gould, 1963

Notorious on campus as the site of the annual watermelon drop during the spring Melon Madness ritual, Harold and Frieda Urey Hall is Revelle College's minimalist masterpiece. Risley and Gould, the same architects who employed pebbled and tiled panels on nearby David Mahlon Bonner Hall, decided on basic concrete for this building.

Urey Hall is named after physicist Harold Urey, who won a Nobel Prize in 1934 for his work with isotopes and who joined the faculty in 1958. The building contains offices and labs for physics and chemistry, including the Keck Laboratory for Integrated Biology II (a satellite of UCSD's Supercomputer Center), the Mass Spectrometric Facility, the Institute for Pure and Applied Physical Sciences, the Protein Crystallographic Facility, and the Biophysics Instrumentation Facilities.

Taking cues from the sun, the architects used large windows on the north side to capture indirect daylight, while limiting the amount of glass on the sun-baked south side. If possible, see this building in the late afternoon, when diagonal shadow lines begin to cut across the building's bold horizontals and verticals, offering proof that in architecture, less can often be more.

8. York Hall

Neptune and Thomas, 1964

Along the eastern edge of Revelle Plaza, Herbert F. York Undergraduate Sciences Building contains chemistry and biochemistry offices as well as biology labs. The arcade along the building's west side, lined with columns that curve up to form Gothic arches, is a place of infinite moods created by forms, light, and shadows.

Wings of the building branch off from behind this arcade at 90-degree angles. In between the wings are courtyards with fountains, one of which has been converted

TOP: *Harold and Frieda Urey Hall*
BOTTOM: *Herbert F. York Undergraduate Sciences Building*

to a cactus garden. Exterior walls feature concrete fins that provide shade for windows behind them.

York Hall is named after Herbert York, UCSD's first chancellor. During the sixties, York was an important player in the creation of Revelle College. York Hall brings together two qualities of its namesake: the scientist and the humanist. On one hand, York was a nuclear scientist who worked on atomic weapons. On the other, he also spent his life as an advocate for peace. York Hall is a simple, rational design, also a sublime and inspiring place, with its ethereal play of light and shadow.

Central Utilities Plant and Cogeneration Plant

9. Central Utilities Plant and Cogeneration Plant
Risley and Gould, Mosher Drew Watson Ferguson, 1963 and 2001

Louvers, vents, and ducts are important design details in this steel-and-glass building. The Central Utilities Plant is finished in green and brown earth tones and blends with surrounding eucalyptuses while pushing puffs of steam skyward. The fenced utility yard in back is an industrial wonder of pipes, boilers, tanks, and valves. If you want to experience UCSD's true life force, here's the place.

The original plant was designed by Risley and Gould. Major renovation including a new cogeneration plan was completed in 2001 and upgraded the old steam-powered chiller, adding to UCSD's on-site energy generation. Mosher Drew's cogeneration plant plugged more juice into the university power grid. The plant earned a Clean Air Award from San Diego Earthworks.

Utilizing efficient, low-emission gas turbine technology, the plant generates 30 megawatts, 80 percent of the campus's energy. UCSD also saves about $250,000 per month by producing its own energy.

In addition to cogeneration, UCSD has in recent years implemented many green features, ranging from paperless offices to hybrid and biodiesel vehicles and a gray water recycling system that produces 122,000 gallons per day for irrigation. By 2009 the university completed a program to update older buildings with energy efficient HVAC, lighting, and control systems.

Future sources of green energy will include a 2.8-megawatt fuel cell that converts methane into electricity and 2 megawatts worth of rooftop photovoltaic solar panels (already on several buildings, including parking structures). UCSD is also considering new technologies to reduce that campus's carbon footprint, such as harnessing seawater to cool buildings and plugging into wind energy.

UCSD's alternative energy sources will produce 8 megawatts, enough to power more than 4,000 homes, reducing carbon dioxide emissions by more than 10,000 tons per year. In 2010 renewable energy accounts for 20 percent of the campus's power; the goal is 30 percent by 2020.

10. Galbraith Hall
Deems Martin, 1965

John S. Galbraith Hall

Decks thrust out like concrete stages where you might find young thespians running lines from *As You Like It* or *Waiting for Godot*. Galbraith Hall is among the most dramatic of Revelle College's modernist buildings, a suitable home for UCSD's Department of Theatre and Dance. One "stage" provides a dramatic entry on the south side; another overlooks Revelle Plaza, one of the busiest public spaces on campus.

The main entry consists of a wide pedestrian bridge across a sunken courtyard. Concrete benches line the entry plaza. Although the architecture maintains the basic proportions and materials of nearby Revelle College buildings, it also has distinctive details. Tapered concrete columns curve up to support the overhanging roof. Eaves bear a pattern of recessed squares.

Galbraith Hall is named for John S. Galbraith, UCSD's second chancellor (1964–1968). A historian specializing in nineteenth-century British history, Galbraith believed that to be great, a university needs a great library, and his wish was granted when UCSD opened its central library (now Geisel Library) in 1970. Prior to the library's opening, the university library was located in Galbraith Hall.

Today, Galbraith Hall is home to CLICS, the Center for Library & Institutional Computing Services, the first UC library to be established in the twenty-first century. The building contains offices, classrooms, a theatrical lighting lab, four rehearsal rooms, and the ninety-nine-seat Wagner Theatre, dedicated in 2008 to the theater department's founding chairman. Wagner obviously appreciated the relationship between architecture and the performing arts. He wrote his thesis on Stanislavsky and Frank Lloyd Wright.

Architects Ward Deems and William Lewis earned architectural degrees from the University of Southern California during the fifties. In San Diego, they are known for significant and dramatic office, military, and medical buildings; several homes; Torrey Pines High School in Del Mar; and the Mormon Temple next to Interstate 5 near UCSD.

With its exciting mix of diagonals, curves, and bold forms, and its dramatic out-door "stages," Galbraith Hall is an excellent example of a design that reflects the shared ideals of Galbraith and Wagner, who both understood the power of architecture to transform human experience.

11. Revelle College Provost Office
Simpson and Gerber, 1967

In the spirit of unassuming military buildings left by the campus's previous military tenants—low, built most of wood, of a scale that did not overwhelm the site—this one-story structure of raw weathered concrete, green glass, and wood trim merges gracefully with the surrounding eucalyptuses and the carpet of fallen leaves and twigs.

Some of Simpson and Gerber's best-known designs are clean-lined La Jolla beach houses covered with rustic wood siding, and the Revelle College Provost Office draws from their residential work. With its modest scale, gabled roof, and lush surrounding landscape, it is an unusually homey and comfortable office building. In the late sixties, when campus administrators faced days full of social and political turmoil, this building provided a safe haven, and it remains one of the most modest and comforting places on campus, quite a contrast to that large urban-scale buildings erected during the decades that followed.

12. *La Jolla Project*
Richard Fleischner, 1984

Richard Fleischner's primal shapes can put the viewer into a timeless state, and it is easy to see why his sculpture is nicknamed "Stonehenge." At foggy dawn or orangey dusk, on rainy days or in the midst of hot Santa Ana winds, UCSD is a place of many moods. The natural environment is enhanced by ubiquitous eucalyptus trees that reflect every change in weather and light. The trees wrap buildings and public spaces like a gray-green blanket that shuts out the world. Fleischner's sculpture rests at the edge of one of the eucalyptus groves. Although this location is only a short distance from the activities of campus life, it feels like a million miles away.

In the years leading up to this work, Fleischner was known for architectural installations using raw natural materials such as hay, sod, grass, and wood. At UCSD, he used seventy-one gray and pinkish blocks of granite (quarried near Providence, Rhode Island, where Fleischner grew up) to create a sculpture resembling ruins of buildings: columns and beams, grouped into entries, arches, thresholds. While some stones are assembled using the standard 90-degree angles of strong construction, one slants at a precarious angle as though a nudge (or an earthquake) might dislodge it.

Fleischner invites the viewer to consider space and form from various perspectives: inside and outside, abstract and figurative, shadow and light, stone against grass, vertical and horizontal.

La Jolla Project was the third public artwork installed by UCSD's Stuart Collection, the public art project that began in 1981. Fleischner's piece is a

TOP: *Revelle College Provost Office*
BOTTOM: *La Jolla Project*

counterpoint to its peers: Niki de Saint Phalle's folksy *Sun God*, near the Faculty Club; and Robert Irwin's elusive *Two Running Violet V Forms*, in a stand of eucalyptus just south of Mandeville Center. Where *Sun God* is widely visible and provides a colorful meeting place for students, and Irwin's installation is a mysterious force field, Fleischner's *La Jolla Project* is a stark and monumental work that resonates with ancient vibrations.

WALK FOUR: MUIR COLLEGE

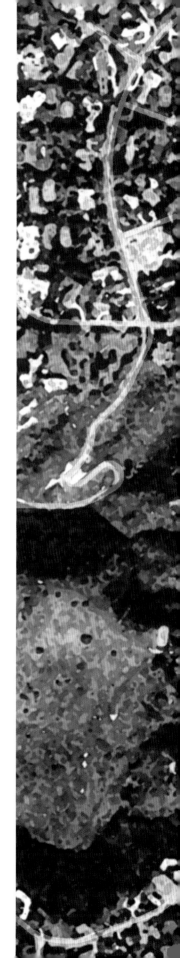

1. Muir Student Housing

Tenaya Hall and Tioga Hall
Dale Naegle, 1969

Tuolumne Apartments
Dale Naegle, 1971

Naturalist John Muir is the name-sake of Muir College, which was UCSD's second college (following Revelle) when it opened in 1967. Its residential buildings for students are named after a lake, a mountain pass, and a meadow in California's Sierra Nevada range. Surrounding a courtyard like tents around a campfire, the buildings form a friendly and inviting neighborhood. On sunny days, students saunter outside to get together with friends, retrieve e-mail, paint banners for Spirit Week, and recharge with espresso from a small cafe.

Architect Dale Naegle was schooled in modernism at the University of Southern California. He is known for his award-winning residential designs, ranging from apartments to spectacular homes. At UCSD, Naegle's courtyard plan

TOP: *Tenaya Hall*
MIDDLE: *Tioga Hall*
BOTTOM: *Tuolumne Apartments*

packs hundreds of dorm rooms and apartments into a compact area that feels spacious and parklike. By building vertical (the high-rise towers) instead of horizontal, Naegle keeps the neighborhood from feeling crowded. Both residential towers utilize double-loaded corridors—hallways flanked by rows of rooms. This plan gives every room an exterior window with a view. Meanwhile, the low apartment building's puzzle-like floor plans make good use of space and give each apartment sufficient windows to provide fresh air and daylight.

At first, these structures make a stark impression with their vast expanses of concrete uninterrupted by decorative details. Spend time here, though, and you will discover how their surfaces change moods in light and shadow, sun and fog, dawn and dusk. Concrete also provides good sound isolation: a party in one room may not disturb a study session in another. Many rooms and apartments have private decks and balconies. West-facing dorm rooms on upper floors even have ocean views. In the courtyard, the landscape contours and concrete planters define semiprivate seating areas that include benches under mature shade trees.

Close to North Torrey Pines Road for easy auto and bus access, and within walking distance of Torrey Pines Glider Port and a beach with great surfing waves, these student housing structures are only five minutes on foot from RIMAC (the Recreation and Intramural Athletic Complex, which includes an auditorium for concerts and other events, as well as gym facilities), the Price Center, and the Geisel Library building.

2. Mandler Hall and McGill Hall
Frank L. Hope Jr., 1969

George Mandler is widely recognized for his research into the mysterious and complex functions of the brain, such as emotion, memory, and creativity. William McGill, UCSD's chancellor from 1968 to 1970, was a mathematical psychologist known for his research into how the brain processes sensory information, such as our responses to light and sound. These two prominent pioneers, together with founding faculty member Norman Anderson, oversaw the building of the Department of Psychology with a shared commitment to research and experimentation. From that foundation, UCSD has become internationally respected for exploring cutting-edge fields of psychology.

UCSD's campus, combining a spectacular site with plans for high-quality new buildings, proved to be an asset in the recruitment of founding faculty members during the sixties. When Keith Brueckner, dean of Letters and Sciences, went to Canada in the mid-sixties to recruit Mandler, he painted an irresistible picture of the campus and its resources. Mandler says, "We were in the post-Sputnik years, and there was money falling out of Washington" as the United States sprinted to stay ahead in the global technology race. UCSD was eager to complete the first campus buildings, but design work was well underway without federal funding.[1] Mandler and McGill were designed as separate adjacent buildings instead of a single structure so that they could be funded in phases. Ultimately, they were built at the same time.

The buildings share the modernist DNA of Muir College: concrete exteriors punctuated by narrow vertical windows divided by protruding fins that soften daylight. According to Mandler, he and his peers joked that with their long, flat arrays of vertical slots, the exteriors resembled IBM punch cards. Upper-level bridges connect these buildings to provide convenient circulation and a different perspective of the campus below. In keeping with the design of colleges throughout UCSD, both buildings have their own shaded courtyards of trees, benches, and elevated planters that

TOP: *Mandler Hall*
BOTTOM: *William J. McGill Hall*

define intimate seating areas. A covered walkway leads past the courtyard to other Muir College buildings.

Architect Frank L. Hope Jr. was introduced to West Coast modernism at UC Berkeley by Bay Area architect William Wurster. Hope's San Diego projects included San Diego Stadium (now Qualcomm Stadium, current home of the San Diego Chargers), Home Federal Savings & Loan, and May Company department store, as well as offices, medical buildings, and residences. Although Hope's buildings often cut a charismatic profile, at UCSD his buildings blend seamlessly in the campus fabric.

3. Applied Physics & Mathematics Building
Mosher Drew Watson Ferguson, 1969

Revelle and Muir colleges marked the beginning of UCSD, but the university's roots reached back to decades of important research at Scripps Institution of Oceanography. Roger Revelle, director of Scripps, brought his creativity and drive to the task of creating a new university campus. Revelle recruited faculty such as Stefan E. Warschawski (founding chairman of the Department of Mathematics) and Keith Brueckner (founding chairman of the Department of Physics). Brueckner, in particular, was attracted to UCSD's philosophy of balancing the arts and sciences to produce well-rounded graduates.

The Applied Physics & Mathematics Building consists of a seven-story tower and a five-story tower connected at the ground level by an open-air hallway and at the upper levels, by pedestrian bridges. Pedestrian bridges also join this complex to Mandler and McGill halls (to the west) as well as to the Humanities and Social Sciences Building (to the south), encouraging a collaborative, interdisciplinary environment. Prominent buildings, such as these two, together with prominent founding faculty, including Bernd Matthias, George Feher, and Walter Kohn, quickly gave credibility to the young university.

The Applied Physics & Mathematics Building is anchored by concrete towers containing stairs and elevators. Like the nearby Mandler and McGill buildings, these buildings are constructed from precast concrete panels (they were cast on site) featuring vertical fins that screen out intense sunlight and provide a private, cloistered interior environment conducive to contemplation and creativity. The panels also contain built-in conduit for mechanical services required by laboratories, such as fume ventilation, power, natural gas for burners, and compressed air. The panels serve as a modular utility system that is easy to alter as interior spaces are reconfigured.

San Diego architect Robert Mosher helped plan the UCSD campus around the idea that each college would have its own identity. As a student of Frank Lloyd Wright, Mosher had experienced the excitement of idiosyncratic architecture. But at UCSD, Mosher designed buildings that are architecturally rich but also harmonious with nearby buildings.

Mosher has been one of the most prolific San Diego architects. The blue Coronado Bridge, designed by Mosher and completed in 1969, arcs dramatically across San Diego Bay. It is one of the region's most visible and stunning public works of architecture. Mosher worked as Wright's on-site architect during the design of the famed Fallingwater house beginning in 1936.

Applied Physics & Mathematics Building

4. Biology Building
Liebhardt & Weston, 1969

UCSD's first biology building, Bonner Hall, opened at Revelle College in 1965. Almost immediately, more space was needed, and the five-story Biology Building brought a significant science population to the heart of Muir College. Muir College's use of planning and architecture to create a communal, collaborative atmosphere is visible in the pedestrian bridge connecting this building to the Applied Physics & Mathematics Building, as well as the landscaped courtyard shared with the nearby Humanities & Social Sciences Building. With its board-formed concrete walls and vertical-finned windows, this structure reflects the distinctive character of the Muir family of structures.

Architect Fred Liebhardt studied at Frank Lloyd Wright's Taliesin schools and worked for San Diego modernist Lloyd Ruocco. Liebhardt's partner, Eugene Weston, the son of an architect, studied at the Art Center in Pasadena. In the late forties, Weston worked for Los Angeles architect Whitney Smith, who was part of the Case Study Houses program of designing simple, affordable modern houses. The Biology Building, with its rectilinear forms and visible structural materials, such as concrete, has the same kind of clarity and honesty as earlier California modernist buildings. Liebhardt and Weston were part of a circle of San Diego architects that also included fellow Muir College architects Mosher, Naegle, and Hope. The group did an admirable job of sublimating individual egos in the interest of designing buildings that together create a cohesive identity for Muir College.

Biology Building

5. Humanities & Social Sciences Building
Richard George Wheeler, 1969

In 1969 Neil Armstrong stepped onto the moon and Woodstock festival, which expressed the arrival of sixties hippie/rock culture, took place. This building, where some of the university's earliest courses on history, politics, and culture took place, opened during a vital year in American history and a critical year for UCSD. The same year, Chancellor John Galbraith recruited scholar, poet, and musician John Stewart to launch the arts and humanities department at Muir College; this building expresses the interweaving of disciplines and ideas, which is central to the college's core values.

Trees and vines intertwine with the architecture, and daylight filters through the trees into lower courtyards. As a result, this seven-story structure is softer and subtler than its nearby siblings. However, it maintains the architectural language of its neighbors with its concrete exterior of narrow vertical windows.

Projecting concrete beams support bridges and walkways in an honest design where structure is openly expressed as a visible element of the architecture. The walkways and bridges move through a changing panorama of architecture, vegetation, and sky. Eucalyptus trees rise past second-floor walkways, providing shade and dappled light. Some of the lower-level beds are landscaped with gravel and boulders that add to the raw aesthetic, while also conserving water.

Outdoor walkways are shaded by precast concrete roofs with a pattern of squares that screens sunlight and adds texture to the surfaces. These shade structures

Humanities & Social Sciences Building

bring to mind the trellises used by early San Diego architect Irving Gill on projects such as the La Jolla Women's Club (1914) and several houses to connect architecture with landscape. In fact, architect Richard George Wheeler had deep roots in California architecture. His father, architect William Henry Wheeler, supervised the development of San Diego's Burlingame neighborhood, made of a collection of bungalows along distinctive pink sidewalks. Like his father, Wheeler earned a degree in architecture at UC Berkeley, a program influenced by a long line of Bay Area architects beginning with Bernard Maybeck, who, like Gill in San Diego, incorporated outdoor spaces—at the turn of the twentieth century, homeowners were still accustomed to the dark, small-windowed rooms of Victorian houses.

Taking a progressive attitude, Wheeler wrote this in an essay titled "Architectural Views":

> Of paramount importance is the necessity for free thinking and not to be bound by conventional or traditional architecture. I do not mean that we are to improve the past, but to study it along with the manner of living in relation to the time in which it was built, is the logical approach. The buildings of the past were designed in relation to the society that was to inhabit them, thus it would be unpardonable folly to associate the present manner of living with the past and to design our buildings based on this decadent [Victorian] style.[2]

After years of evolution as a part of the curriculum at Revelle, Muir, and other UCSD colleges, Social Sciences became a unified division in 1986 that today includes nine academic departments and numerous interdisciplinary programs. The Division of Social Sciences is one of the largest academic divisions at UCSD.

6. Mandeville Center
A. Quincy Jones and F. E. Emmons, 1975

Bare concrete walls and surrounding redwood trees have weathered well for this monument to the brutalist style. While this building is "brutal" in its uncompromising minimalism and hard edges, it also proved to be a versatile, durable, and adaptable home for UCSD's Department of Visual Arts and Department of Music through their

The Ernest W. Mandeville Center for the Arts

formative years (in 2009 the Department of Music moved to the new Conrad Prebys Music Center).

The Mandeville Center's sawtooth roof provides rows of north-facing skylights that spill soft daylight into studios and offices. Primary circulation is outdoors, along wide concrete walkways shaded by overhangs, taking advantage of San Diego's mild climate. Breezeways cut through the center of the building, connecting the building to the surrounding campus and dividing the long, solid concrete building into friendlier dimensions. Offices and studios surround lower-level courtyards, which give each room direct access to daylight and fresh air.

The 800-seat Mandeville Auditorium was designed to accommodate a variety of performances and is a comfortable venue that has presented memorable artists ranging from David Sedaris and the Kronos Quartet to Ravi Shankar, as well as countless dance, jazz, and world music concerts. Mandeville has also been a venue for performances of work by members of the renowned Department of Music faculty, such as compositions by the department's founders Will Ogdon and Robert Erickson. Fans of abstract expressionist art, Japanese architecture from the same era, or San Diego's modernist icon Irving Gill are sure to connect with Mandeville's raw sculptural jolt.

Perhaps the most extraordinary thing about the building is that it inspires creativity: it has accommodated world-renowned faculty composers and visual artists, and it has produced hundreds more prominent, often experimental, artists. During the early years of the music department, Mandeville Center also had a romantic allure: on many days, the sound of live music from classes and practice sessions drifted through the building. Meanwhile, the Department of Visual Arts makes good use of courtyards as outdoor studios and temporary installation spaces. Each academic year, outdoor spaces fill with sculptures of wood or metal or found objects, and installations of wire or string or masking-tape hieroglyphics suddenly appear.

Original Student Center

7. Original Student Center
Paul McKim & Associates, 1972

Like the functional military build-ings where UCSD began, the original student center is a modest wood and stucco complex tucked beneath mature trees in a mellow corner of campus. Even a cursory exploration of this area of campus will make one aware of UCSD's sixties origins. The complex includes a used bookstore, an organic food co-op, the campus radio station (KSDT), and newspaper (*The Guardian*), as well as an espresso cafe with a wood deck surrounded by greenery as lush as something out of *Jurassic Park*. The architectural sophistication is in the way these buildings define outdoor spaces by their placement, and through the use of walkways, courtyards, and decks. Scattered around San Diego are low-key modernist homes by McKim in the same tasteful, organic style. The heart of the campus shifted many years ago to the Price Center, with its bold forms, large bookstore, and food court. But there are those at UCSD who still prefer the rustic wood buildings of the early years.

8. Student Center Expansion
Public Architects, 2006

Outdoor public space is as vital to the university's life as its buildings. This light, graceful addition to the original student center included changes to the surround-ing circulation plan to create new pedestrian connections from Mandeville Center to the old Student Center's shops and to points south. Wide new steps lead down from Mandeville's southern plaza to a courtyard behind the newly expanded Student Center, so that it is no longer necessary to take a circuitous route from Mandeville Center to the Student Center. Low concrete walls provide seating next to trees set in beds covered with patterned cast iron grates that pick up the plaza's rhythm of squares and rectangles while echoing the rustic look of the original center. The new building is a long, narrow two-story structure about the same length as Mandeville Center. It also echoes the center's proportions and redwood-strip detailing, which, in turn, makes a visual connection with the redwood walls of the old Student Center. A second-level deck runs along the north side of the addition, providing outdoor circulation while shading a concrete platform added along the edge of Mandeville Center's plaza. The platform's edge is a great place to sit outdoors while people watching or sky-gazing. The most dramatic stroke here is the roof, which ramps up at a slight angle to accent the east end of the building, offering a visual hint of the spicy Thai food at the restaurant below. The roof covers a tall, open, glass-walled space containing both a student lounge and the restaurant.

Student Center Expansion

Lesbian, Gay, Bisexual & Transgender Resource Center

9. Lesbian, Gay, Bisexual & Transgender Resource Center
Public Architects, 2006

Established in 1999, the Lesbian, Gay, Bisexual & Transgender (LGBT) Resource Center took its symbolic place as a significant campus institution when it moved to an attention-getting new building of its own. It was an architectural step out of the closet. Connected to the new Student Center by an elevated steel-and-redwood walkway, the LGBT Resource Center building is a freestanding oasis featuring private courtyards enclosed by block walls with creeping vines that weave in and out of openings between the blocks. It utilizes the same proportions and same basic materials as the Student Center expansion designed by the same architects: concrete, redwood, and steel, with aluminum windows.

The building provides offices as well as spacious meeting rooms that look out on the serene green courtyards at each end of the building, which function as a buffer between this structure and the day-to-day bustle of the campus. Instead of conventional concrete or grass, the architects (with input from landscape architects Spurlock Poirier and the artist Robert Irwin, whose work is represented in the campus's Stuart Collection) landscaped these courts using perforated pavers with tufts of grass poking through the holes. This landscaping technique saves on both maintenance and water.

Architects Jim Brown and Jim Gates of Public Architecture have done construction work on many of their buildings and have a fondness for salvaged and industrial materials assembled with careful attention to detail. They are known as hands-on architects (on projects this big, of course, construction is handled by commercial contractors). This aesthetic is apparent at the LGBT building in the simple aluminum awnings suspended from steel cables, horizontal redwood strip cladding attached with uniform rows of screws, and the upper windows covered with transparent screens printed with gigantic images of grasping hands and, on the east end of the building, Wonder Woman.

10. Main Gymnasium
Liebhardt & Weston, 1968

Basketballs pound a beat accompanied by sneaker squeaks during spirited games in these bare-bones gyms favored by old-schoolers who like gritty, sweaty, no-frills workouts. These buildings along Ridge Walk are as solid and functional today as they were when they first opened. Over the years, the Main Gym has hosted not only great collegiate and recreational basketball games, but also, in the sixties and early seventies, emotional gatherings of students, faculty, and administrators.

The Main Gym's zigzag folded-plate concrete roof energizes the front of the building, accommodates skylights over the lobby, and gives an interesting geometry to the basketball gym beneath it. Broad steps lead to wide banks of entry doors beneath textured concrete walls. The walls are divided by concrete pilasters that branch out at

Main Gymnasium

the tops, where they meet the overhanging roof. On rainy days, the overhang shelters visitors. Inside, a long, skylit atrium leads to the basketball court. Telescoping bleachers retract to provide room for half-court games. Second-level exercise balconies equipped with gym mats and equipment, as well as weight lifting and cardio-fitness machines, offer exercisers a view to basketball games while they work out. On the building's north side, a concrete walk leads to the entrance past a row of first-floor rooms for fitness classes such as spinning and yoga. With their raw concrete showers, steel lockers, and tiled restroom floors, the locker rooms transport you back to a time of purely functional fitness facilities. Next to the Main Gym, the smaller Recreation Gym (1973) is available for sports that do not require bleachers for spectators and has windows and skylights that bring natural light to the basketball courts.

11. Natatorium
Liebhardt & Weston, 1967

Post-and-beam construction is a simple but solid system of vertical posts and horizontal beams tied together for maximum structural integrity. This spare, modern method, popularized by the experimental Case Study Houses program in Los Angeles and developer Joseph Eichler's tract housing, gained currency throughout Southern California during the fifties and sixties. The influence of Los Angeles modernism is visible throughout San Diego and in many buildings at UCSD. The Natatorium is a spare, elegant design, with beams tapered like airplane wings, light streaming through window walls and skylights, and shade provided by deep roof overhangs. The building takes on the day's changing light, reflected both indoors and out, which casts intricate reflections and shadows from the surrounding eucalyptus trees. Compared with a swim at the larger, newer, outdoor Canyon View Recreation Center across campus to the east, a workout here is a more serene experience in the grottolike space.

12. Green Faculty Club
Mosher Drew, 1987

Shaded by mature eucalyptus trees and surrounded by a dense drought-tolerant landscape, the Ida and Cecil Green Faculty Club does not call attention to itself. Esoteric conversations fill the air at lunchtime as administrators, faculty, VIPs, and a variety of visitors gather for the comfortable, collegial atmosphere and the casual buffet. Members and their guests dine at tables in the large, open dining room or on the outdoor terrace or courtyard. Banquet-size spaces and smaller meeting rooms accommodate a range of special events, including weddings and bar/bat mitzvahs,

TOP: *Natatorium*

BOTTOM: *Ida and Cecil Green Faculty Club*

wine tastings and author readings, faculty and staff retirement parties, and holiday soirées.

A gabled standing-seam metal roof with deep eaves, eucalyptus-gray wood framing that blends with the nearby trees, and panoramic windows that frame blue-sky views impart a feeling of a Sierra ski lodge, a style of which Mr. Muir would no doubt approve. The foyer, dining rooms, and meeting rooms look out on landscaped courtyards with umbrella-shaded tables. Skylights line the roof's peak, spilling natural light into the dining room.

When this building was designed, the nation was still in the grip of postmodern architecture, with its gaudy colors and kitschy combinations of classical details. UCSD hired one of the region's most seasoned, well-respected architectural firms, one that did not buy into trendy designs. Since Robert Mosher had consulted on the original campus master plan, the architects were also very familiar with UCSD and its somewhat rustic natural setting. They designed this building in deference to this unique natural environment and location, and to provide a casual and inconspicuous retreat for faculty, administrators, and their guests.

Taking cues from its predecessor, the expansion designed by M. W. Steele Group and completed in 2006 combines wood beams, a gabled metal roof, large windows, and an open floor plan in a building as inviting as a mountain lodge. As a counterpoint to the original building's right angles, Steele used curvilinear forms, as with the concrete privacy wall that wraps the structure's northwest corner. The foyer, dining rooms, and conference rooms afford views of landscaped courtyards with umbrella-shaded tables.

Old and new plantings merge in a richly varied drought-tolerant landscape of greens, grays, and earth tones accented by seasonal color, proving that one can create a fantastic California garden and still conserve water. Plants range from Asiatic jasmine to Leopard plants, clivias, variegated lily-turf, Pittosporum, Raphiolepis, and New Zealand flax. Native plants include coffeeberry and lemonadeberry, as well as strawberry trees.

13. *Sun God*
Niki de Saint Phalle, 1983

When it was lowered into place by a crane in January 1983, *Sun God*—a twenty-nine-foot sculpture consisting of a concrete arch supporting a brightly colored fiberglass bird—became the first piece in UCSD's Stuart Collection of public art. The morning after *Sun God* was installed, someone had left a large handmade paper egg with the greeting "Happy Birthday" at the sculpture's base. Overnight, the piece had been adopted as a campus mascot.

Before she created *Sun God*, artist Niki de Saint Phalle, who was born near Paris, had modeled for *Vogue* and other high fashion magazines during the late forties, studied theater and acting in Paris, and began painting in the mid-fifties, with an interest in the work of Rousseau, Picasso, and the Spanish architect Gaudi. In the sixties, she made "target" paintings by shooting holes in assemblages of materials, and in the late-sixties her "Nana" sculptures depicted female figures in papier-mâché, yarn, and cloth. Around the time she began work on her piece for UCSD, she also released her own perfume.

Sun God evokes opposing ideas: pleasure/fear, dream/nightmare, cartoon character/serious work of art. In the midday sun, the big bird comes across as an amusing totem to blue skies, green grass, and lazy, carefree days. In the shadows of dusk or dawn, however, this same bird looms like a gigantic monster or primal god, with a beaked face, spiky gold crown, and wings raised as if to protect his or her territory.

De Saint Phalle had scouted the campus by helicopter and identified a location just south of where the Ida and Cecil Green Faculty Club would open in 1987, but she had not marked the specific spot on the expanse of grass. When it came time to pin down her site, she was in France, and it fell to the Stuart Collection's Mathieu

Sun God

Gregoire to decide where the piece would stand. When Gregoire visited the site to make a decision, he came across a couple stopped on the lawn. The woman was carrying a parrot. When she set it down on the lawn, Gregoire decided that was where *Sun God* would go.

Gregoire supervised the construction of de Saint Phalle's concrete arch. The fiberglass bird was fabricated in France, shipped to Long Beach, California, and trucked to UCSD, where the sculpture has become the most visible and best known (on campus) of the Stuart Collection's pieces. Students gather at the well-known icon—sometimes in the middle of the night. Couples have been married there. Over the years, the bird has been dressed in a cap and gown and accessorized with dark glasses and headphones. Offerings have been left beneath the arch, like a ritual out of a sci-fi movie. As the Stuart Collection's first piece, *Sun God* set a high standard by achieving that elusive merger of mass appeal and quirky creativity. In 1984 students organized the first Sun God Festival, and it has become an annual rite of spring, attracting thousands.

WALK FIVE: THURGOOD MARSHALL COLLEGE

Marshall College Administration Building

1. Marshall College Administration Building
Kennard, Delahousie & Gault, 1978

African American, Native American, and Mexican American student activists mobilized in 1967 to demand a voice in planning UCSD's new Third College. They demanded a program that would educate from a multicultural point of view. Armin Rappaport, a history professor, was hired from UC Berkeley to become Third College's founding provost. But the process was just beginning. Who would run the college? What courses would be offered? What would it be named?

Controversial figures joined the stormy debate among administration, faculty, and students. Professor Herbert Marcuse, an avowed Marxist, spoke out in favor of the multicultural, politically diverse curriculum advocated by student groups. So did his philosophy student, budding activist Angela Davis, who believed that the mission of the new college should be "to provide Black and Brown students the knowledge and skills we needed in order to more effectively wage our liberation struggles."[1]

Those were not ideas one would hear from Republican Ronald Reagan, who became California's governor in 1967, or William McGill, who became UCSD's chancellor in 1968. Both were conservatives committed to the status quo (traditional Euro-centric curricula and America's significant commitment of dollars and soldiers to the Vietnam War). Reagan's antipathy toward student activists came to a head in 1969 when he dispatched the National Guard to UC Berkeley to break up huge crowds of students and activists gathered in support of a People's Park on state land.

At UCSD, plans for a Third College became formal in 1965 when an administrative committee issued its proposal. The college's muse would be Clio, the Greek goddess of history. Its mission would be a balanced mix of sciences, arts and humanities. But as student activism against the Vietnam War and for minority rights gained strength, student activists at UCSD demanded a much different multicultural approach that would address the needs of minority students.

"We demand that the Third College be devoted to relevant education for minority youth and to the study of the contemporary social problems of all people," read the written demands presented in March 1969 to the administration by the Black Student Council and the Mexican American Youth Association. "To do this authentically, this college must radically depart from the usual role as the ideological backbone of the social system, and must instead subject every part of the system to ruthless criticism. To reflect these aims of the college, it will be called Lumumba-Zapata College."[2]

Patrice Lumumba was a Congolese activist and Emiliano Zapata was a Mexican revolutionary. Deciding on the new college's name became almost as difficult as deciding on its academic direction. By the time the new Third College opened in the fall of 1970, administrators had rejected the name but altered the curriculum to provide a broader, multicultural education. In 1993 the college was renamed in honor of African American Supreme Court Justice Thurgood Marshall. A bronze bust of Marshall marks the entrance to Thurgood Marshall College Administration, which faces Ridge Walk, a primary north-south pedestrian promenade.

The Marshall College Administration Building is a modest one-story structure that provides an intimate, friendly environment for interaction between administration, faculty, and students. The tan stucco building is a well-proportioned composition of cubic shapes, configured to invite visitors into and through the building. Wide glass entry doors, a lobby with a skylight and hardwood floors, and another set of doors at the back of the lobby connects three central spaces: entry courtyard, lobby, back courtyard. Most offices have windows with views of the lush landscape that pushes up against the building. In the back courtyard, umbrellas shade colorfully tiled tables. The courtyard is surrounded by a rolling landscape and mature trees, including broad eucalyptus. Just beyond the courtyard, to the north, is artist Francisco Zuniga's small sculpture *Yucateca Sentada*, which depicts a kneeling Native American woman glancing to one side as if to discover what lies ahead.

African American architect Robert Kennard, a principal of Kennard, Delahousie & Gault, earned his architecture degree from the University of Southern California in 1949, when it was Southern California's leading center for modernist architecture. Kennard worked for prominent architects Richard Neutra and Victor Gruen, as well as Robert Alexander, who drafted UCSD's first campus master plan and designed early buildings.

In the spirit of Kennard's role models, the administration building—constructed during a period of tight university budgets—is a clean, modernist design that is subtly and smartly interconnected with the landscape and the surrounding Marshall College plan.

The modest, timeless building is a fitting headquarters for a college founded on the democratic ideal that all Americans (and UCSD students) deserve to be heard and represented. Over the years, the building has been the site of grassroots dialogues that helped Marshall College embody the ideals of Justice Thurgood Marshall.

"We continue to uphold our founding principles of social responsibility and access to excellence through diversity, justice, and imagination," reads the plaque beneath the bronze bust of Marshall. "Thurgood Marshall College maintains a commitment to the development of both the scholar and the citizen."

2. Social Sciences Research Building
Kennard, Delahousie & Gault, 1976

Thurgood Marshall College was forged through heated discussions among administration, faculty, and students, and the dialogue continues as the school matures and offers a changing array of social-sciences courses. At the core of Marshall College's curriculum is a sequence of classes (known as "Dimensions of Culture")

Social Sciences Research Building

that provides undergraduates with a broad spectrum of viewpoints and teaches them critical thinking and writing skills.

Sheltered by mature trees including Marshall College's signature acacias, the three-story Social Sciences Building is barely visible from Ridge Walk. The building is sited on a gentle slope to the east of this central thoroughfare. The building is configured in a wide V and tucked into the slope, with two stories visible on the uphill (Ridge Walk) side and three stories visible in back (on the east side).

The building cuts a long, low profile on its gently sloped site. Off-white stucco walls create interesting forms and define interior and exterior spaces. Horizontal lines give exterior walls the appearance of wood siding, and the lines reinforce the building's horizontal masses. On each level, exterior walls project forward or step back to provide shade or create balconies, and the building's beveled corners add an interesting dimension.

The building's plan reinforces the alignment of Marshall College's walkways and buildings, which run along diagonals, against the grain of the predominant north-south/east-west campus grid—in the same way the college was founded against the grain of traditional academia. The site plan produces triangular and trapezoidal outdoor spaces, which are used as seating nooks, courtyards, and landscaped beds. The building contains more than thirty research labs and support spaces, offices, study rooms, and meeting rooms.

While some campus buildings are extroverted designs that express the raw excitement of the learning and cutting-edge research that takes place within, the Social Sciences Research Building takes a different approach. It is a modest building that blends with the landscape to merge seamlessly into its neighborhood.

3. Cognitive Science Building
Kennard, Delahousie & Gault, 1976

Set in the eucalyptus grove between Library Walk and Ridge Walk, at the heart of Thurgood Marshall College, the Cognitive Science Building is the largest and most visible of the college's early buildings. It anchors the center of the Marshall College neighborhood.

Designed to complement the nearby Social Sciences Research Building, the Cognitive Science Building contains about fifty research labs and support spaces, offices, classrooms, and meeting rooms. Interdisciplinary research projects bring together teams of philosophers, linguists, psychologists, computer scientists, anthropologists, sociologists, and neuroscientists, who explore the phenomena of intelligence, thought, and behavior.

The building features long horizontal forms emphasized by horizontal lines in the stucco and long balconies. Long, low forms in off-white stucco angle away from the

Cognitive Science Building

predominant grid of the campus plan to align with Marshall College's diagonal roads and walkways. The building and landscape fit neatly in the middle of the Marshall College site plan.

Each side of the Cognitive Science Building features distinctive forms that respond to its context. On the north side, a brick courtyard provides a landscaped outdoor lounge. The courtyard opens to a wide walkway between this building and the Social Sciences Research Building.

On the east side, where Geisel Library and Price Center are visible in the distance, a pedestrian path runs beneath a steel shade trellis. As the path turns to follow the structure's south side, it is punctuated with copper-roofed pavilions that match the copper awnings. Stair towers anchor the corners. The towers feature sections of glass block that let natural light into stairwells. Horizontal banks of windows run the length of the building, bringing daylight inside.

The mature landscape around the building includes acacias, pines, eucalyptus, and other trees. The trees provide plenty of shade for courtyards and outdoor seating areas. Low, drought-tolerant shrubs offer green views from first-floor offices as well as heightened privacy.

Cognitive science was a building block of UCSD's curriculum in the early sixties and has become one of the university's most popular majors. At UCSD, cognitive science research has produced a variety of breakthroughs. Some are known mostly among academics and scientists. Others have become the subject of bestselling books such as faculty member Don Norman's *Emotional Design* (2003), which explores the design of everyday objects and our responses to them. Since the early years, UCSD's Department of Cognitive Science has grown into various buildings beyond Marshall College, but this building stands as the humble stage where many early scientific dramas played out.

4. Marshall Lower Apartments
Wong & Brocchini, 1975

On many afternoons, music pumps from the windows of the Marshall Lower Apartments, and barbecue smoke drifts from balconies and patios into the surrounding eucalyptus grove. Although Marshall College is part of one of California's largest

Marshall Lower Apartments

universities, the apartments exemplify UCSD's founding strategy–inspired by Oxford and Cambridge universities–of creating a campus subdivided into a collection of small colleges, where new students can have a sense of security and community while having access to all the benefits a large university offers.

Marshall Lower Apartments are located east of Ridge Walk and north of the college's central cluster of buildings. For undergraduates settling into college lives, the location is one of the most inviting and convenient on campus. The complex also includes the Fireside Lounge–a student gathering place in a separate building–a basketball court, and a parking lot to one side.

The apartments are five minutes on foot from key campus destinations, including the Geisel Library, the RIMAC Center (for recreation and concerts), the Price Center, and a significant number of undergraduate classrooms.

Apartments are grouped in tan two-story buildings with rust-colored metal awnings. Most apartments are three bedrooms, but there are a few one-story, one-bedroom units. The five buildings are designed around courtyards, so that every apartment cluster has an intimate outdoor space, and each apartment gets natural light from several directions. Apartments feature large corner windows that make the interiors feel more spacious, and buildings are shaded by mature trees, including pines and eucalyptuses. The trees and low shrubs provide a buffer around and between buildings in a neighborhood that is only a short walk from the center of campus, but seems a million miles away.

5. OceanView Terrace

Delawie Bretton Wilkes Rodrigues Barker Associates, 1988

There are many spectacular views at UCSD, but as its name suggests, OceanView Terrace offers some of the most spectacular: students can watch sunsets over the Pacific Ocean while they dine on some of the university's best food. Walls of glass provide panoramic views from every table in the dining room, especially along the curved walls that push out from the building's west side. There are additional tables on an outdoor terrace that faces the ocean. A student lounge on the top floor provides equally spectacular views.

The building's east side, along Scholars Drive, is a spare expanse of concrete. The other three sides feature decks and covered walkways, which connect the building to the landscape and allow visitors to experience the fine weather. Steel balcony railings surround transparent wire mesh panels (instead of solid railings) that maintain panoramic views. In the tradition of regional Southern Californian architecture, some of the most important rooms here are outdoors.

Stucco, glass, awnings, and accents in an oceanic gray-green palette relate the building to its natural context. Broad steps descend through the landscape to a rolling lawn that is a perfect place to read, sleep, or savor a picnic lunch among blossoming coral trees and flowering shrubs. In this prominent location, this thoughtfully designed building brought new elegance to Thurgood Marshall College.

OceanView Terrace

WALK SIX: ELEANOR ROOSEVELT COLLEGE AND NORTH CAMPUS

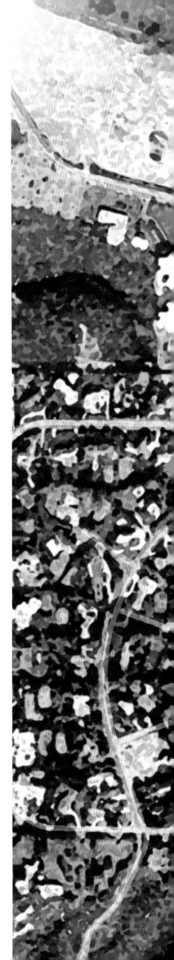

A Singular Vision

In the course of his forty-year career, architect Moshe Safdie has won wide acclaim for projects that range from experimental housing to the Skirball Cultural Center in Los Angeles and the National Gallery in Ottawa, Canada. Only a few architects ever have the opportunity to plan and design a new college from scratch. Eleanor Roosevelt College is the only college at UCSD masterminded by a single architect, from siting and neighborhood planning, to architecture, materials, and addressing budgetary requirements. The project also let Safdie collaborate with his daughter Taal and her husband Ricardo Rabines, San Diego architects who joined the design team.

When it opened in 1988, Fifth College did not have its own campus. Classes were held in a variety of UCSD buildings. The college was named for Eleanor Roosevelt in 1994 (the then–First Lady Hillary Clinton gave the keynote address), and Safdie's new campus was completed in 2003. The goal was to provide a curriculum with a global perspective. Undergraduates are required to take a two-year core sequence of classes, known as "Making of the Modern World," that gives a broad perspective of history.

Enrollment has grown from 390 the first year to 3,500 today. Along the way, Roosevelt expanded into a patchwork of spaces scattered around campus. Safdie's plan brings the college together into a distinctive and inviting neighborhood. The college occupies a rectangular fourteen-acre site overlooking architect Louis Kahn's landmark Salk Institute, the Torrey Pines Glider Port, and the Pacific Ocean. Included are residence halls, apartments, computer labs, conference rooms, administrative offices, a five-level parking structure, the International House (programs and services for international students), and two prominent public buildings: Café Ventanas and the Great Hall.

The site is bounded on the west by North Torrey Pines Road and on the east by Ridge Walk, the pedestrian promenade that runs north-south across the UCSD campus. Roosevelt College is bisected by Scholars Lane, with rows of buildings on either side organized around two significant public spaces: a narrow pedestrian plaza (east of Scholars Lane) and a big lawn known as The Green (west of Scholars Lane).

Along North Torrey Pines Road, Roosevelt College is visible as an orderly row of four-story student housing blocks in the college's signature materials: yellowish stucco, horizontal aluminum bands, and aluminum windows. In the past, UCSD sited buildings away from the campus's edges. This was partly because campus expansion was focused around the central library for several years after it opened in 1970 in the middle of campus. Another reason that UCSD only began defining urban edges in recent years is that surrounding land was not intensely developed until the eighties and nineties. Before that, there was no contextual logic for urban development along the campus's perimeter. Along the western boundary of Roosevelt College, buildings line North Torrey Pines Road, separated only by a sidewalk, giving UCSD a more visible presence in the community.

The uniform scale and architectural design of buildings at Roosevelt create a cohesiveness not found at other UCSD colleges, where buildings were designed by several architects over a period of years. Landscaped public spaces tie the Roosevelt community together. Safdie's arrangement of housing along pedestrian walkways and his inventive placement of entrances, courtyards, porches, and balconies create a strong sense of neighborhood—thanks to the plan, students who live and study here bump into each other by accident all the time. Most apartments and residence hall rooms look out on landscaped courtyards and plazas. In contrast to the tall student housing towers at Muir and Revelle colleges, the low-rise student housing at Roosevelt nestles into the landscape instead of towering above it. This inviting garden neighborhood has become one of the most popular places to live at UCSD.

Otterson Hall (Rady School of Management)

1. Otterson Hall (Rady School of Management)
Ellerbe Becket, 2008

(Otterson Hall is not part of Eleanor Roosevelt College. It is part of UCSD's North Campus, but is included here as a convenient stop on your Roosevelt tour.)

In the new millennium, fast-moving breakthroughs in technology, bioscience, and other emerging enterprises prompted the need for new kinds of business training. The Rady School of Management was created to groom new leaders for new international companies. Many of its students are already established professionals. They come to Rady to gain entrepreneurial skills. At the core of the Rady curriculum is a "lab-to-market" series of classes in which graduate students launch new startup companies. The building provides an efficient learning environment with a corporate edge, bridging the gap between the academic and business worlds.

The school is named for Ernest Rady and the Ernest Rady Family Foundation, which contributed $30 million to the school—the second-largest philanthropic gift in UCSD history. (The total cost of the $43 million building was funded entirely through private donations.) Otterson Hall, the school's headquarters, is named for William

Otterson, founder of UCSD Connect, a program that brings together entrepreneurs, scientists, and other innovators to create new local companies.

The four-story building is configured in two wings: a long main section that runs east-west and looks like a giant metal-and-glass bird, and a smaller rectangular block behind it, to the north. The main building is clad in alternating bands of greenish glass and aluminum. The base and other areas are covered with StoneLite panels that resemble natural sandstone but are lighter, less expensive, and extremely durable. Open terraces occupy the pointed tips of the bird "wings." The building contains offices, classrooms, conference rooms, and common areas, and is wired for high-speed networking and videoconferencing.

Courtyards, terraces, and outdoor seating areas enhance the building's upbeat, entrepreneurial vibe and encourage spontaneous interaction and collaboration. Tucked between the building's two sections is a courtyard with rows of palm trees in circular beds. The perimeter is landscaped with gray-green drought-tolerant plants that follow the craggy terrain. South of the building, a pedestrian path crisscrosses a slope through a landscape of native plants.

In the spirit of its entrepreneurial programs, Otterson Hall incorporates cutting-edge green features including natural ventilation, a combination of natural light and energy efficient light fixtures, office chairs made from recycled material, and low-emitting, recyclable building materials. Rooftop solar panels provide an 18-kilowatt boost, part of a campuswide initiative that will eventually generate 500 kilowatts of electricity with rooftop panels.

2. RIMAC (Recreation and Intramural Athletic Complex) and RIMAC Arena
Parkin Architects, 1995

Comedian Robin Williams has stalked the RIMAC arena stage, delivering his manic brand of humor. UCSD's women's basketball team has competed in the Division II West Regional Tournament inside RIMAC, and indie rock bands like Controlling the Famous have performed at the annual Winterfest celebration. On RIMAC's athletic field, President Bill Clinton delivered the keynote address at UCSD's 1997 commencement, followed in 1998 by Newt Gingrich.

This is a typical season for UCSD's RIMAC, a multipurpose complex that includes a flexible 5,000-capacity arena, as well as the university's prime recreation center, arrayed with treadmills, recumbent bikes, free weights, weight machines, and rooms for all sorts of workouts.

The arena is situated behind the recreation complex, with its own entry plaza on the building's north side. Wide landscaped steps along the building's north wall provide sunny seating areas at the plaza's edge. Ticket windows are set to the side

RIMAC (Recreation and Intramural Athletic Complex) and RIMAC Arena

of the tall glass entry atrium, which has several sets of double glass doors. Smart planning here prevents human traffic jams.

UCSD fields competitive teams in basketball, volleyball, badminton, and other sports. RIMAC Arena is a versatile venue with retractable bleachers, a sprung wood sports floor that serves as a shock absorber for athletes, and ten retractable glass basketball backboards. It serves athletes ranging from varsity competitors to philosophy majors and medical students who play lunch-hour pickup games.

The site slopes down to the east from Ridge Walk. A tree-shaded plaza leads to the recreation complex and its glass box entrance. Exterior walls consist of colored and textured concrete masonry. Walls of glass give exercisers great views of the dense, mature landscape. Green steel trellises shade the outdoor spaces. Concrete steps and benches provide a variety of seating options.

3. Hopkins Parking Structure
Esherick Homsey Dodge and Davis, 2008

(Hopkins Parking Structure is part of UCSD's North Campus but is included here as a convenient stop along your Roosevelt tour.)

Rooftop solar panels tilt their faces toward the sun, transforming the 1,400-space Hopkins Parking Structure into a significant source of power. By shading the parking lot's concrete, the panels also prevent heat island effect—the combined radiation from sun-baked surfaces in urban areas can raise air temperature significantly. Perched atop steel trees, the panels create a man-made forest that looks great from a distance, makes a visual connection with the nearby eucalyptus grove, and shades parked cars on a hot day.

Hopkins Parking is a prime example of UCSD's drive for energy-efficiency. The rooftop "grove" of twenty-eight solar panels generates 537,000 kilowatt hours of electricity annually, enough to power forty-five homes. Additional green features include erosion-resistant landscaping around the structure, low-wattage lighting, and the structure's convenient location along the campus shuttle bus route.

TOP: *Hopkins Parking Structure*
BOTTOM: *San Diego Supercomputer Center Office Addition*

Located at the corner of Hopkins Drive and Voigt Drive, the seven-level parking structure features a cement plaster-and-glass elevator tower and open steel stairs, landmark features visible from a distance. The first-floor corner is occupied by parking management offices. Perforated steel panels enclose the structure, softening the visual impact of all the cars. Lightwells bring daylight to lower levels, making them pleasant and secure.

4. San Diego Supercomputer Center Office Addition
Gwathmey Siegel & Associates, 1996

In 1984, the year of George Orwell's famous book and David Bowie's song, Apple introduced the first Macintosh computer. The following year, the San Diego Supercomputer Center (SDSC) opened, with its Cray XM-P supercomputer that resembled a round red Naugahyde bench from an airport lounge. UCSD became one of a handful of universities with supercomputer capability, and the impact was enhanced by the campus brain trust of world-renowned scientists, engineers, and researchers who actually knew what to do with the XM-P.

When the needs of the center outgrew the facilities available in its original build-ing, a long, narrow five-story office wing was added in front. With its Neutra-like front facade of white stucco, aluminum panels, and horizontal bands of glass, the addition gives the center a sleek identity along busy Ridge Walk.

Offices line the building's north side, where horizontal banks of square windows provide soft northern light. Stairwells, restrooms, copy rooms, and conference rooms are on the south side. These rooms do not demand daylight, and the minimal number of windows reduces interior heat gain, which cuts utility bills. Conference rooms are located in a black tile tower that protrudes from the building.

With its smart floor plan of daylight-filled offices conveniently close to common areas and conference rooms, the building provides researchers with private office space for focused individual work as well as larger rooms for group collaboration and brainstorming.

5. San Diego Supercomputer Center East Expansion
EHDD Architecture, 2008

Processing power is what launched the San Diego Supercomputer Center, but the newest addition was prompted by a drive to develop and promote "cyberinfrastruc-ture," the combination of computers, data archives, networks, software, and digital instruments that allows computer and processing power to be harnessed for real-world work.

The architecture is inspired, in part, by the high-powered computer equipment for which the building was designed. It combines a sleek, light-colored exterior of cement plaster, concrete, and glass with an open, flowing interior that gives glimpses of high-tech equipment and all the activity around it.

The site slopes down east of Ridge Walk, south of the original Supercomputer Center and north of Hopkins Parking Structure. Tucked into the slope, the five-story center has two underground levels. Two wings project perpendicularly to the east from the main building, like long square tubes that soar into space and come to rest on concrete columns. The ends of the wings are glass, looking out across a eucalyp-tus grove. The sides are lined with narrow horizontal windows. Aluminum sunshades protect south-facing windows from direct sunlight.

The East Expansion is set behind a line of street trees, a curved driveway, and a landscaped plaza along Hopkins Drive. The plaza leads between the building's wings to concrete steps to the second-level main entry.

San Diego Supercomputer Center East Expansion

Inside are classrooms, research labs, offices, larger rooms for collaborative work, a 200-seat auditorium, a visualization lab, and a 7,000-square-foot supercomputer machine room. To create a culture of interdisciplinary collaboration, the interior is organized into "research neighborhoods," with offices arranged around flexible meeting and circulation spaces. Chance collisions and conversations are a vital part of the creative process.

Given the energy consumption and heat gain associated with intensive data processing, EHDD Architecture went to great lengths to make this building a green prototype for technology-based businesses. UCSD was the first university to join The Green Grid, a global consortium of information technology companies dedicated to energy-efficient data centers.

The building incorporates Low-E glass (specially treated to reflect sunlight and to insulate interiors), steel-trellis sunshades, exposed concrete interiors that help keep spaces cool, and a solar-reflecting roof. Interior finishes are nontoxic, and the building also incorporates fly-ash concrete. (Fly ash is a by-product of coal-burning energy, and concrete made from it flows smoothly during a pour and requires less water. Because it is denser than regular concrete, it also lasts longer.) Furthermore, offices are naturally ventilated, and where possible, daylight is a primary light source.

A system called CoolFlex makes the cooling system operate efficiently by isolating the cooling equipment from the hot-air exhaust. The building gets its power from the campus's natural gas cogeneration facility. Additionally, the Supercomputer Center East Expansion includes energy-saving CRAH (Computer Room Air Handler) ductwork, and high-efficiency power supplies that save more than a half-million kilowatt-hours per year compared with previous units. Sensors throughout the building measure energy consumption and thermal effectiveness, providing useful information for future building designs.

All of this "greenery" earned the building a Silver rating from the LEED (Leadership in Energy and Environmental Design) Green Building Rating System as well as a Best Practice Award from the Higher Education Energy Partnership, for innovative heating, ventilation, and air-conditioning. In this building, UCSD lays claim to more computer storage capacity than any university in the world: twenty-five petabytes (Google processes about twenty petabytes each day). Like other UCSD buildings, including Atkinson Hall, the Supercomputer Center is connected to an ultra-fast broadband network that is a prototype for the next-generation public Internet. It is used for research and is funded by the National Science Foundation.

Social Science Building

6. Social Science Building
Gwathmey Siegel & Associates, 1995

Gwathmey Siegel was known during postmodernism's eighties heyday for accenting modernist forms with cones, curves, and cylinders inspired by classical architecture. This same eclecticism is on view at UCSD.

The building faces Ridge Walk, with the front facade divided into three sections, each stepped back slightly farther from Ridge Walk. Square windows are set in white- and gray-tiled projections. Along the ground floor, walkways lead beneath the building to elevators and outdoor corridors. Behind the building, stair towers rise from the centers of circular brick courtyards between the building's wings. The courtyards are the building's focal points, with tall palm trees in circular beds echoed by circular wood benches and circular tables. The slope below the courtyards is landscaped with orderly arrangements of succulents, dry grasses, and other drought-tolerant plant materials. A bridge of wood and weathered steel spans the slope from north courtyard to Hopkins Parking Structure, with its rooftop grove of solar panels.

Robinson Building Complex (Graduate School of International Relations and Pacific Studies)

7. Robinson Building Complex (Graduate School of International Relations and Pacific Studies)
Kaplan/McLaughlin/Diaz and Clark Beck and Associates, 1990

West of Ridge Walk, the Robinson Building Complex takes the form of a triangle; along Ridge Walk, the building's base is defined by a short rectangular wing next to the round auditorium building. The triangle's other two sides consist of long rectangular wings. At the triangle's center is a terraced circular courtyard with steps and walkways that make connections to surrounding structures.

In the south wing are the Graduate School of International Relations and Pacific Studies (IR/PS) Library, a computer lab, classrooms, and a student lounge. The north wing contains administrative offices and a conference room. The 175-seat auditorium along Ridge Walk is the site of frequent important lectures and symposia related to political, social, and entrepreneurial issues faced by the San Diego region and Pacific Rim countries such as Japan and China. Large circular vents at various points along exterior walls contrast with the building's bold squares, rectangles, and triangles. A high level of craftsmanship is visible all around, from the precise grout lines of Jerusalem stone tiles that cover the building in earth-toned horizontal bands, to the circular plaza's curved concrete terraces and walls.

Outdoor circulation is key to the building's open, inviting appeal. Steps and paths lead in and out from the courtyard between landscaped edges of buildings. On the west side of the courtyard, sliding glass doors lead from the central plaza through the building to a tree-shaded deck on the west side. These sliding doors bear a translucent map of the world.

The complex houses the Center on Pacific Economies, the Center for U.S.–Mexican Studies, and the Institute on Global Conflict & Cooperation. Among issues considered in recent years were China's "one-child rule," which has created a shortage of young people to support an aging population; North Korea's drive toward nuclear weapons; and the global implications of President Obama's economic plan.

With its angular forms and circular center, the Robinson Complex is an apt metaphor for the global issues we face amid infinite and challenging intersections of cultures, traditions, business practices, and politics.

8. Café Ventanas
Moshe Safdie and Associates, 2003

Café Ventanas caps the north end of The Green, Eleanor Roosevelt College's grand, parklike open space. The cafe and the Great Hall at the south end of the Roosevelt campus are siblings with swooping wood-beamed roofs and sweeping glass walls. Sitting at a table in Café Ventanas is a little like sailing aboard a nineteenth-century vessel. Curved roof beams resemble the ribs inside a hull, and glass walls angle to a prowlike point.

Behind the dining room, students load their plates from a long, U-shaped buffet that offers a selection of foods including organic fruits and vegetables, sushi, and French fries (no trans fats!). A circular light well and round columns lead visitors along the buffet line. A low wall separates the buffet from the dining room, where wood tables rest on a gray tile floor and potted palm trees add an exotic touch.

The second level is dedicated to the dining room and buffet area. Storage and maintenance facilities are tucked out of sight on the building's first floor, and the third contains offices and conference rooms.

Café Ventanas is a social hub of Roosevelt College, and not just at meal times. Tables on the second-floor terrace in the shade of the overhanging roof are great for studying. Broad steps lead down to The Green. They create informal bleachers for watching Frisbee sessions or softball games.

9. Cuzco House East and West
Moshe Safdie and Associates, 2003

Architect Moshe Safdie designed Cuzco House East and West as a cozy collection of apartment buildings arranged along the north-south pedestrian plaza. The plaza is a lush, tree-lined public space through this portion of the Roosevelt campus. Cuzco

TOP: *Café Ventanas*
BOTTOM: *Cuzco House East and West*

contains one-to four-bedroom apartments. The buildings are configured in parallel wings flanking a courtyard. They are connected by a fourth-story bridge containing apartments.

Buildings are tucked into the sloped site, with subterranean gardens outside lower rooms. Exteriors match Roosevelt's predominant scheme of off-white stucco, horizontal aluminum bands, and square aluminum windows. Concrete benches in the courtyards are magnets for students—they can sit and log onto the campus wireless network, play guitars, or sip coffee as their peers roll past on skateboards and bicycles.

Cuzco's neighborhood of student housing provides a lush and secluded parallel reality that's a million miles away from campus reality yet only a few minutes from essential UCSD destinations.

Mesa Verde Hall North and South

10. Mesa Verde Hall North and South
Moshe Safdie and Associates, 2003

There's something faintly Italian about Mesa Verde Hall, a student apartment complex along a pedestrian mall between Ridge Walk (on the east) and Café Ventanas (on the west). The apartments are arranged in parallel wings lining the pedestrian mall. As at the Cuzco apartments, the wings of Mesa Verde are connected by fourth-story bridges that contain apartments. The bridges are reminiscent of those between buildings along Venice's canals.

The exterior of off-white stucco, square windows, and horizontal band of aluminum lends a latter-day Renaissance look, like the basic forms and banded exteriors of Italian architect Palladio's buildings. Cypress trees along the building add to the Italian sensibility.

Safdie made sure that all of Roosevelt's buildings—especially student housing— connect with grand outdoor spaces. Walking anywhere within Roosevelt is a pleasant garden experience.

Broad steps descend toward the apartments from Ridge Walk. The steps are flanked by concrete terraces landscaped with low drought-tolerant plants and tall grasses. The buildings and one of the bridges form a square arch above the wide entrance to Mesa Verde's courtyard, lined with elevated beds defined by low concrete walls that provide built-in seating.

Great Hall

The north and south wings of the four-story Mesa Verde complex contain thirty-eight student apartments. South-facing apartments are shaded by aluminum awnings, and all apartments have windows that swing open to capture coastal breezes.

Mesa Verde Hall gives students a calm, secluded enclave within the well-organized Roosevelt neighborhood. In turn, Roosevelt College makes strong connections to the surrounding UCSD campus. This hierarchy of expanding social circles is just the thing for fledgling students adjusting to life at the Big U.

11. Great Hall
Moshe Safdie and Associates, 2003

Like Café Ventanas, the Great Hall is a bold public building that anchors one end of Eleanor Roosevelt College. The uses of the two buildings may be different, but they're a matched set of forms and materials, with walls of glass, ceilings supported by curved roof beams resting on round white columns, and landscaped public spaces that serve as outdoor rooms.

The Great Hall caps the south end of the pedestrian plaza lined with student apartment blocks. Located near the Pangea Parking Structure, the Great Hall is used for banquets, conferences, celebrations, and various special occasions. It is only a short distance from Ridge Walk and several academic departments that utilize the spacious room for special events.

On the east side, the building's main entrance is a brick courtyard landscaped with a grid of flowering trees. To the west, at the intersection of Pangea Drive and Scholars Drive North, the Great Hall's sharp, jutting corner is a memorable feature. The building is configured as a wedge, with a curved north-facing window wall that takes in ocean views and gentle northern daylight.

One night, the hall was set up for an event celebrating global unity. The decor included tabletop tents bearing likenesses of historical figures ranging from Bob Marley to Napoleon Bonaparte. It was a colorful, truly international occasion, and one could imagine that the curved roof beams were inspired by Japanese teahouses, while the columns referenced ancient Rome, and the smooth stucco walls reflected Latin America or Spain.

12. The Green

Moshe Safdie and Associates, 2003

At the heart of Eleanor Roosevelt College, Safdie's Green is a huge lawn that plays Central Park to a few hundred students living around its perimeter. The Green is a football field-size lawn crossed by diagonal sidewalks and dotted with trees, inspired by grand outdoor spaces such as Harvard Yard at the famed Ivy League university. Sidewalks also run along the lawn's edges, next to landscaped beds in front of apartment and dormitory buildings. Gray steel lampposts line sidewalks, and keep them secure and inviting at night.

Café Ventanas, the student-dining hall with its sweeping roof, anchors The Green's north end with amphitheater-like steps that descend to the lawn. At the

The Green

south end is a student lounge with tables and vending machines, with sliding doors that open onto The Green. Midway along The Green's east side, steps between nearby apartment buildings culminate at a brick landing that overlooks the park-like space. Steel picnic tables on the landing are a great place for dining al fresco, brown-bag style. In between housing blocks to the west of the lawn, open areas with tall trees bring late afternoon sunlight to The Green, adding stripes of gold between long dark shadows that cross the lawn.

13. Institute of the Americas, 1984
Gildred Center for Latin American Studies, 1994
Copley International Conference Center, 1995
Tucker Sadler and Associates

UCSD's only significant architectural nod to the region's Spanish roots is this U-shaped courtyard complex, with its white walls, red-tile roofs, and tiered fountain. San Diego's obsession with Mediterranean styles began with Mission San Diego de Alcala (in the area known today as Mission Valley), built by Spanish Franciscans in the eighteenth century as part of their mission to Christianize the Native American population. San Diego's heritage of Mediterranean architecture is also visible in buildings such as the Casa de Bandini in Old Town, the Spanish Colonial buildings in Balboa Park, and legions of tract houses.

The Institute of the Americas represents a California variation on Spanish architecture known as Monterey style, named for the California city where it originated. In the 1830s, Boston merchant Thomas Larkin built a two-story white adobe home in

Institute of the Americas

Monterey. The house had a gently slanted roof, which shaded second-level balconies. In the ensuing years, the Monterey style, distinguished by courtyards, simple white stucco walls, second-level balconies, and wood or wrought-iron railings, was used for a variety of California buildings, ranging from houses to restaurants.

UCSD's use of Monterey style reflects the institute's mission of promoting U.S. relations with Latin America (as well as Canada). Given San Diego's border location, relations with Mexico are a high priority.

The building is configured in a U-shape around a courtyard that is open on the west side. This broad outdoor space provides a dramatic entrance from the west, where steps lead past a low white stucco wall framed by palm trees. The courtyard is surfaced with pebbled concrete squares outlined by bands of red concrete. A fountain bubbles at the center, as water spills over a stack of three circular basins into a concrete Mediterranean pool.

Along the courtyard's eastern edge, the Institute of the Americas building features Monterey-style second-level decks with wood railings. The decks are set between the building's brick columns. French doors are framed, Spanish style, with dark wood set into the stucco walls. To the south, the one-story Copley International Conference Center's red-tile roof overhangs the building to rest on square columns, providing shade for visitors. To the north, the Gildred Center for Latin American Studies is a similar one-story structure.

In addition to the courtyard entry on the west side, the Institute of the Americas also has an entrance on the east side, where the site slopes down from Ridge Walk. A footbridge extends from the pedestrian promenade to the building's second-level entrance. Large trees flank the bridge. Dark wood window frames alternate with brick pilasters in an orderly rhythm.

The institute was founded by Theodore Gildred, a developer and former U.S. ambassador to Argentina, in collaboration with former UCSD chancellor Richard Atkinson. Its mission includes facilitating networking and the exchange of ideas, forming public/private partnerships, and developing policies for managing economic growth in Latin America. Projects related to energy and technology are a high priority.

WALK SEVEN: WARREN COLLEGE

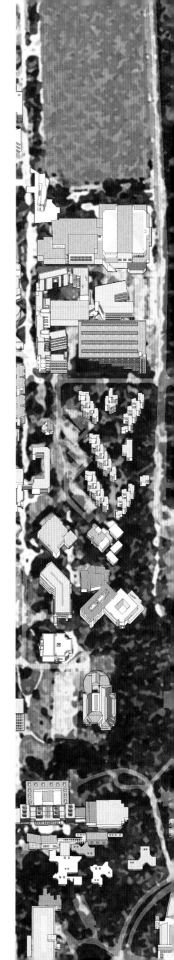

Jacobs Hall (Engineering Building Unit 1)

1. Jacobs Hall (Engineering Building Unit I)
Buss, Silvers, Hughes & Associates, 1990

Heading east from the heart of campus and onto Warren Mall, a wide pedestrian mall that runs from Geisel Library through the center of Warren College (named after U.S. Supreme Court Chief Justice Earl Warren), the first visible building is Jacobs Hall, the eight-story headquarters for the Jacobs School of Engineering. The Jacobs School is concentrated around the mall, a broad space with a landscape that ranges from open lawns to intimate seating areas defined by trees and planters. The monumental scale of the mall and buildings makes it easy to spot. The scale also represents the Jacobs School's status as one of the university's most prestigious programs, where significant research takes place in many vital specialty areas.

Jacobs Hall is a bold and versatile structure that serves an impressive array of purposes. The building contains classrooms, lecture halls, offices for faculty and graduate-level researchers, and research facilities including an optics lab. It also contains the Center for Wireless Communications and the Cymer Center for Control Systems and Dynamics. Special structural features include vibration isolation to protect sensitive equipment and clean rooms (spaces free from dust and contaminants) for delicate research.

Concrete sections alternate with expanses of reflective glass. The plan consists of a long main building from which four smaller wings project to the south at 90-degree angles and with landscaped, below-grade courtyards between the wings. Translucent awnings shade rows of windows on each floor. At the ends of each wing, narrower four-story sections look out on the mall. All offices are contained in the wings. While the main building's laboratories require air conditioning, the offices are naturally ventilated, an early example at UCSD of sustainable design in a technically demanding structure.

Flexibility is essential in science buildings as technology advances and research methods evolve. In its first two decades, Unit 1 has proven to be the engineering school's workhorse. It houses a constantly changing collection of research programs. Like other campus buildings, it receives an occasional update to its exterior. In 2009, an enclosed entry was added at the building's base.

The Jacobs School is named for engineer and entrepreneur Irwin Jacobs, a former UCSD professor who founded communications giant Qualcomm. Jacobs and his wife, Joan, have contributed more than $100 million to the school. The school has some of the highest-ranked graduate engineering programs in the world and includes six departments: Bioengineering, Computer Science and Engineering, Electrical and Computer Engineering, Mechanical and Aerospace Engineering, NanoEngineering, and Structural Engineering. Some of the technology developed at UCSD is utilized by Qualcomm and other leading communications companies. State-of-the-art facilities help attract the finest faculty and graduate-level researchers in the world. This building was the first in a new generation of buildings that have given the school its proper place on campus.

2. Powell-Focht Bioengineering Building
Anshen + Allen Architects, 2002

Powell-Focht is a concrete-frame building of two wings that angle along the edges of Warren Mall and the Academic Court. The Academic Court is a landscaped courtyard enclosed by Powell-Focht and two other buildings—Atkinson Hall and the Computer Science and Engineering Building—that line its perimeters. Together the three buildings nearly doubled the square footage of Jacobs School of Engineering.

Named for famed engineer Charles Lee Powell and late San Diego Superior Court Judge James L. Focht, Powell-Focht was the first of the three. The Academic Court, with its angular hardscape, diverse plantings, and artist Tim Hawkinson's *Bear* sculpture, is a parklike space that unites these buildings into a neighborhood. Powell-Focht's north wing provides a low horizontal edge to the Academic Court. Walls on this side of the building are bluish sandstone, a natural material that works well with the courtyard's stone surfaces and landscaping. Near the building, the courtyard features seating areas of concrete benches amid rows of palm trees.

Along Warren Mall, Powell-Focht's concrete-and-glass forms echo the blocky vertical forms of Engineering Building Unit I next door. Expanses of glass are shaded by perforated aluminum awnings that provide protection from harsh southern sun.

Powell–Focht Bioengineering Building

Every year, research here produces important discoveries that lead to new treatments for human ailments, including cancer, immune system disorders, malfunctioning genes, and the effects of aging and injury on bones, ligaments, cartilage, and muscles. Offices and labs are clustered to encourage collaboration across disciplines.

The ground floor includes an open atrium lobby, administrative offices, classrooms, and a 150-seat lecture hall that lets out to an intimate outdoor space at one edge of the Academic Court. The basement contains flexible open spaces that can be used for various collaborations with private industry. A fourth-floor library opens onto a terrace, and the basement contains a large vivarium. The building also houses the William J. von Liebig Center for Entrepreneurism and Technology Advancement, which works with scientists and entrepreneurs to figure out how new technologies can lead to profitable companies.

At the heart of the structure is a 150-seat lecture hall equipped for interactive video conferencing and multimedia presentations. Each of four floors is dedicated to a specialty area: biotechnology, biofabrication, instrumentation, and *in vivo* technology. Each discipline has specialized spaces, such as tissue culture labs and a machine shop.

Powell-Focht was constructed almost entirely with private donations. As a bold landmark to cutting-edge research, it has proven to be extremely valuable in recruitment, and it has also been an asset for introducing prospective new donors to the exciting work taking place at the Jacobs School.

3. Warren Academic Quad
Spurlock Poirier, 2007

Warren Academic Quad is a public space for the three buildings that surround it: Atkinson Hall, the Powell-Focht Biongineering Building, and the Computer Science and Engineering Building. Roughly the size of a football field, it is a popular location for receptions, graduations, and even outdoor lectures.

Landscape architect Andrew Spurlock was inspired by a dynamic plaza at the University of Michigan that is cut by diagonal lines. This courtyard also utilizes strong diagonals, and each building is sited to reinforce the dynamic site plan. Unlike many others groupings of buildings, these are not set at 90-degree angles. Two primary diagonal axes crisscross the court. One connects the Computer Science building with Powell-Focht; the other leads from Warren Mall through the Academic Court to Atkinson Hall. Landscape materials—concrete, stone, ground cover, trees—define the courtyard's forms, a mix of right angles, curves, and diagonals.

Significant funding for Atkinson Hall came from private donations, including supporters who purchased commemorative bluestone (a type of sandstone) bricks for a prominent central pathway in front of the building. Each donor has a brick bearing his or her name.

Spurlock and Poirier collaborated with the architects for all three buildings around the Academic Court so that each building transitions smoothly to the central space. Each building has its own semiprivate outdoor space at the edge of the court, and each of building's outdoor space picks up key materials, textures, or colors from the building. Trees, hedges, and grasses help define these spaces. Along the edge of the Computer Science building, for instance, redbud trees set in gravel beds bloom magenta in spring, near tables interspersed with low hedges. In front of Powell-Focht, King palm trees outline a series of seating areas with low concrete walls.

Atkinson Hall's shade trellis separates the building's entrance from a pedestrian tunnel that leads under the building to student housing on the other side. Atkinson does not have its own semiprivate outdoor seating area like the other two buildings, but it is close to an espresso cart. You could spend a day in the courtyard investigating its many different spaces, taking stock of the diverse materials and plantings, and communing with Hawkinson's bear, the centerpiece of Academic Court. The complex design evokes the complexity of cutting-edge research. The *Bear* reminds us that the creative process requires a sense of lightness and humor.

4. *Bear*
Tim Hawkinson, 2005

Some art works at UCSD are baffling, causing visitors to scratch their heads, ponder awhile, and move on without any great revelations. Hawkinson's *Bear*—a part of the Stuart Collection—has the opposite effect. This giant sculpture evokes immediate grins. After all, what could be more appealing than a teddy bear basking in the sun?

Except, when you take a close look at the 23-foot 6-inch bear, he is an ominous creature: a rolling, life-threatening avalanche, as monumental and mysterious as the pyramids. You wonder how these eight granite boulders got here, and what holds them together in their precarious arrangement. Although they could be something

Warren Academic Quad

lightweight and fake from a movie set, the truth is, if the boulders suddenly tumbled, you would be crushed by 370,000 pounds of granite.

Hawkinson selected the boulders from a site near Pala Indian Reservation in northern San Diego County. The bear's torso—the largest boulder—was transported to UCSD aboard a truck that normally carries space shuttle parts. The boulders were inched into place by cranes, a process that took several days. They are held together by steel embedded deep in the stone, to meet earthquake-safety codes.

There is irony in the idea of a huge stone bear who reminds us of a stuffed animal but looks as if he could live in a national park. He is not soft and cuddly, and his construction took significant amounts of planning and engineering. Despite the calculating and conniving required to seat the boulder on its base, the mechanics are not what come to mind when you see him. His rough Ice Age skin contrasts with the sleek aluminum, steel, and glass of nearby buildings while his soft, organic forms are the opposite of the courtyard's acute angles. Hawkinson's *Bear* may look like an innocent stack of stone, but it is an artwork as deliberate as any other in the Stuart Collection. The precise placement of raw, unaltered boulders and the monumental scale of a childlike fantasy figure force one to look more closely—and perhaps differently—at him and at the architecture around him.

Conceptually, *Bear* is an important element in the Academic Court. Given the large size of the plaza, its scale would become intimidating without the bear as its appropriately scaled sentry.

5. Atkinson Hall
NBBJ, 2005

When it opened with a spectacular nighttime multimedia event in the Academic Court nearby, Atkinson Hall generated the kind of buzz usually reserved for a Hollywood premier. Since the opening, the buzz has become more of a global hum. Companies ranging from film director George Lucas's Skywalker Ranch to Qualcomm dispatch emissaries to Calit2 on a regular basis. (Atkinson Hall is known around campus as "Calit2"–"Cal-I-T-2"–since it is the home of the California Institute for Telecommunications and Information Technology.) They want to learn about the newest in twelve-channel audio, broadband video distribution, motion-capture systems, and other technologies with potential applications in movies, video gaming, cell-phone communications, computers, aerospace, defense, and more.

Calit2 represents a new paradigm for research and education, a multidisciplinary center that sustains the vision of UCSD's founders, who believed in the intersection of the arts and the sciences. Calit2 is a think tank where engineers, scientists, computer programmers, composers, video artists, musicians, and other elite researchers collaborate.

Atkinson Hall combines the most advanced technologies with some of the university's most exciting architecture. The building is an angular wonder of steel and glass near two other new engineering buildings. Together, the three buildings–Atkinson Hall, Powell-Focht Bioengineering, and Computer Science and Engineering–define the Academic Court at their center. Inside, Atkinson Hall contains some of the world's most advanced research facilities including clean rooms for nanotechnology,

Bear

Atkinson Hall

micro-electro-mechanical labs, immersive virtual reality, and an ultra-high-definition digital cinema. If you wonder where technology for the next generation video game will come from—the one where Arnold walks right out of the screen and grabs you by the neck—this might be the place.

The six-story building is configured to encourage collaboration and facilitate interdisciplinary projects. Offices are on the front side and consist of open cubicles, so that co-workers can easily see and communicate with each other; the back contains open work areas that encourage collaboration. It also consists of a tall glass wing of offices, labs, research areas, and other spaces; and a low horizontal wing enclosed in concrete, metal, and stone, with minimal glass except on the side facing the Academic Court. The low wing includes a 200-seat auditorium with ultra-high-resolution video, 3-D sound, stereo imaging, and telepresence conferencing. Atkinson Hall also contains a flexible "black box" theater that adapts to a variety of performances, several conference and meeting rooms wired for audio and video, and offices for faculty, staff, and grad students. Also located here are the HD Broadcast Studio, the Audio Spatialization Lab, the Performative Computing Lab, the Virtual Environments Lab, the Computer Experiment Lab, and the CRCA (Center for Research in Computing and the Arts).

The building's elusive forms reflect the mysterious, futuristic research conducted by its nine hundred occupants. UCSD scientists and researchers wanted a transparent building that could be easily reconfigured, with materials that do not impede wireless communications. The building is covered with phenolic-resin-fiber panels that allow Wi-Fi waves to pass through. Each side of the building is tailored to views, sun exposure, and wireless reception. Even the back and sides of the building are thoughtfully designed and landscape. Unlike buildings where the front gets all the excitement and other sides become neglected alleys, all sides of Atkinson have equally exciting forms and materials. Like new entertainment technologies, it offers a true 3-D experience.

Asymmetrical arrays of narrow vertical bay windows add to the building's amorphous, unconventional appearance. Rectangular and trapezoidal forms contrast with the curved back wall. Tapered beams, railings, concrete walls, and other components pick up the diagonal lines of the courtyard and building.

There are few 90-degree angles inside the building—a tour is a trip through unpredictable spaces, like the research that takes place here. Scientists write cryptic messages on whiteboards lining the corridors.

Inside the lobby and elsewhere, narrow slots in the walls give a sense of looking out through a circuit board. To one side of the lobby is a gallery for installations such as media artist and activist Carlos Trilnick's *Anti-Personnel Mines Project* (2009), a temporary multimedia installation that called attention to the "insidious nature of land mines," according to the artist's introductory text that was displayed on the gallery wall.

Green features include a computer system that controls every light switch in the building so that lights turn off when they are not needed. The system is part of an energy-conserving package that makes Atkinson Hall one of the most energy-efficient buildings on campus. Other green ideas at Atkinson Hall are more basic. Calit2 donated 150 ceramic cups to employees to reduce paper-cup waste. Employees are trained to turn off computers and printers when not in use (workers tended to leave them on overnight for fear of missing software updates or information backups, but these functions now occur even when computers are off overnight). And employees and researchers are encouraged to rely on digital documents instead of paper copies.

Atkinson Hall has earned wide recognition. It was awarded a Grand Orchid by San Diego's Orchids & Onions program, in which the public votes for its favorite and least favorite buildings.

6. Computer Science and Engineering Building
Bohlin Cywinski Jackson, 2005

In the new millennium, Jacobs School of Engineering has emerged as one of UCSD's prime centers for research and new technology. For its range of forward-looking, collaborative breakthroughs, the school has earned an international reputation as a leading think tank.

The Computer Science and Engineering Building sits at the edges of the Academic Court and combines elegant administrative offices for Warren College with dynamic, colorful offices, labs, classrooms, and meeting spaces dedicated to Computer Science and Engineering. Areas of instruction and research include bioinformatics and computer engineering, education and research programs in computer vision, graphics, embedded systems and software, and cutting-edge work in networking and cryptography. Courses include image rendering, computer gaming, and wireless mobile systems.

Within the building are two hundred offices, forty-four research labs, eleven conference rooms, a high-tech auditorium equipped for multimedia and teleconferencing, and a room where female students and faculty can breastfeed their infants, designed in cooperation with the student group Women in Computing.

This building's concrete-and-glass wings define a corner of the Academic Court, the likeable *Bear* sculpture. Where the two wings intersect, a glass-walled main entrance is indicated with a circular, translucent awning high atop the building. Metal columns wrapped with conical sheets of steel lead to the entry. Lots of glass and big skylights bring daylight into the wood-paneled atrium lobby, where open stairs slant upward through a wide, circular opening. From one corner of the lobby, a long wood-paneled hallway leads into the administrative offices for Warren College.

The influence of computer science has expanded vastly in recent years, affecting many specialty areas in technology and sciences. The Computer Science and Engineering department's significant collaborations include those with the San Diego Supercomputer Center and with the California Institute of Telecommunications and Information Technology. Scientific breakthroughs create new business opportunities, which in turn create jobs. Students enter their programs as ambitious researchers and scientists. By the time they leave, many of them are positioned to make major contributions at leading companies, and to launch new companies of their own.

Computer Science and Engineering Building

7. Warren Residential Halls

Delawie Bretton Wilkes Associates, 1993

Perched on a canyon's edge at a far corner of campus, Warren Residential Halls are as close to nature and as far as one can get from the chaos of campus life while still living on campus.

Warren Residential Halls

Designed at a time when postmodernist architecture had nearly run its course, the cluster of tan stucco five-story buildings has strong modernist roots, but with bright green and red trim that one does not see in new designs today. Courtyards and balconies line narrow walkways that feature trees as tall as the buildings. Sand volleyball courts are only a few steps away, as are a small concrete amphitheatre and the student dining facility.

At heart, Delawie Bretton Wilkes are old-school modernists who believe in putting function before form. They are known for carefully considered, clean-lined designs that respond to client needs and site conditions. Homer Delawie, the company's founder, studied architecture at California Polytechnic State University in San Luis Obispo, worked in the office of Lloyd Ruocco (who designed UCSD buildings including the Munk Laboratory at Scripps Institution of Oceanography), and opened his own San Diego office in 1961. Along with Robert Mosher, Fred Liebhardt, Frank L. Hope, Jr., Hal Sadler, and others, Delawie was of the generation of postwar San Diego architects who did not receive much national attention but who were known within their profession for modernist designs on a par with some of the best work produced by their more famous peers in Los Angeles.

8. Canyon Vista Administrative and Dining Facility
Delawie Bretton Wilkes Associates, 1993

A sibling of the architects' Warren Residential Halls, this project provides students with spectacular views from dining rooms and outdoor terraces. Tucked into a slope at the lip of a canyon, it features the same tan stucco with bright green and red accents that lend it an Italian flair.

The complex is organized around a central courtyard open on one side of the canyon. Circulation around and through the building is mostly outdoors via stairs and sidewalks shaded by green and red steel trellises. Some surfaces are paved with concrete in a pattern of red and green squares.

Between this building and the Warren Residential Halls to the north is a small, semicircular concrete amphitheater next to a brick plaza planted with jacaranda trees that bloom with violet flowers in the spring and summer.

Canyon Vista Administrative and Dining Facility

Thanks to its outdoor-oriented design, the building makes the most of its canyonside setting. Rabbits scurry out of the bushes to take a look around. Hawks drift overhead, scanning the canyon for a snack. Leaves rustle in afternoon breezes that often flow through the canyon.

9. Engineering Building Unit II

Zimmer Gunsul Frasca Partnership, 1994

Anchoring the east end of Warren Mall, Engineering Building Unit II serves as the engineering school's Arc de Triomphe, capping the end of a grand pedestrian boulevard like the Parisian arch punctuates the end of the Champs Elysées. This red-tiled arch—the front of the building—joins the two wings of the building and leads to a courtyard of clay-colored gravel under the second- and third-level pedestrian bridges (they offer great bird's-eye views). In the courtyard, a low stone wall curves toward an elevated bed with jacaranda and palm trees, bronze flax, and a compact carpet of grass. The perimeter is lined with red-flowering bougainvillea that climbs the building's concrete walls.

Radiating from the entry arch, the two wings feature front facades with a zigzag pattern of window bays that heightens the contrast between smooth concrete and green glass. The building's side walls are straight planes of concrete textured with a corduroy pattern. Along Unit 2's west side, a wide pedestrian walk runs between this building and the back of the adjacent Computer Science and Engineering Building. Lining the edges of this walkway are low hedges and concrete walls that define

Engineering Building Unit II

elevated beds of trees and low shrubs. Dedicated to mechanical and aerospace engineering, Unit 2 contains offices, classrooms, research labs, and specialized functions such as the Center for Energy Research.

The back of the building also receives special attention. Balconies serve as outdoor hallways, with open steel-and-cable railings, and sections of wire mesh screen that cut some of the sun's glare and soften this side of the building's appearance.

The combined effect of Warren Mall is that the outdoor environment in this part of campus is a grand and cohesive public space that helps bring together people from various disciplines.

Unit 2 is not as glitzy as the newest engineering buildings, nor is it as spare as UCSD's early modernist buildings. Instead, Unit 2 is a refined, spirited design that smartly merges indoor and outdoor spaces while making friendly connections to campus.

10. Warren Lecture Hall and Literature Building
Liebhardt Weston and Associates, 1990

The primary purpose of a university is education, and an essential requirement for a campus is plenty of classrooms and lecture halls. Warren Lecture Hall is ground zero for undergrads taking foundation arts and humanities courses, such as literature, philosophy, math, music, and history. It includes the Department of Music's Studio A, where countless CDs by UCSD composers and performers have been recorded. The Literature Building houses administrative offices for the Division of Arts and Humanities, as well as other offices for faculty, staff, and teaching assistants.

Liebhardt Weston and Associates, which also designed the High Bay Physics Lab and the Natatorium, the campus's first swimming pool, are among a few San Diego architecture firms responsible for most of the first- and second-generation buildings at UCSD. Their designs are a testament to following the tenets of rigorous, practical modernism.

The lecture hall and literature buildings are steel, glass, and concrete blocks. Both buildings use skylights and banks of windows to gain natural light. The lecture hall building is configured around a courtyard that gives fresh air and green views to the offices and classrooms surrounding it. In the literature building, most

Warren Lecture Hall and Literature Building

upper-level offices and conference rooms have excellent views of the campus, the natural landscape, and distant developments beyond campus.

Mature plants look luscious and lively against the buildings' pale gray walls. The fragrant landscape includes flowering ground cover, ferns, and shade trees in the courtyard and next to walkways.

11. Powell Structural Systems Laboratory

Leonard Veitzer, 1986

Vices and Virtues

Bruce Nauman, 1988

Powell Structural Systems Laboratory is the centerpiece of a three-building cluster of structural labs in this part of campus. To the south are the Powell Structural Components Lab and the High Bay Physics Lab. With its 55-foot ceiling and 120-foot-long interior span, Powell Lab is the largest of the three and is able to accommodate sections of bridges and roads.

Powell Lab is named for Charles Lee Powell, an engineer who invented and patented new methods for building concrete structures. Powell's ideas were utilized in the design of much of the early infrastructure in Los Angeles. When Powell died at age 96, his will called for the creation of a nonprofit foundation that has since contributed millions of dollars to engineering research.

In 1989, the 7.1 magnitude Loma Prieta earthquake socked the San Francisco Bay Area, dislodging a 50-foot, 250-ton section of the San Francisco Bay Bridge. Elevated freeways collapsed and many buildings were damaged. In the months following the earthquake, UCSD's labs were booked solid as government and transit agencies and private contractors began searching for new earthquake-safe methods of construction.

Inside Powell Lab, engineers apply earthquake-size forces to freeway sections, columns, and girders to determine which forces cause failures, and which materials and designs can withstand these forces. Scientists from Powell Lab often collaborate with researchers from UCSD's Supercomputer Center, which houses hardware and software for visualization, high-speed computing, and simulation modeling.

Applying research conducted at UCSD, the California Department of Transportation (Caltrans) developed a system to retrofit bridges by wrapping their piers in steel. In the years since the Loma Prieta earthquake, many highway bridges throughout the state have been retrofitted. Another technology that came out of testing at UCSD is a carbon-fiber material used to reinforce stone columns in historic structures. Research at Powell also has applications in national security, such as

TOP: *Charles Lee Powell Structural Systems Laboratory and* Vices and Virtues
BOTTOM: *High Bay Physics Laboratory*

systems to monitor structures like San Diego's Coronado Bridge and new ways to protect buildings from bomb blasts.

UCSD earthquake guru and bridge engineer Frieder Seible, dean of the Jacobs School of Engineering, supervised the structural testing of components for a new San Francisco–Oakland Bay Bridge to replace the old span that suffered structural failures during the 1989 earthquake. During slow-motion "pseudodynamic" tests, bridge components were pushed by huge, pistonlike mechanisms that simulate the movements and forces of an earthquake. Tests for the new Bay Bridge span focused on welded joints. These joints include fasteners developed at UCSD that function as "fuses" in an earthquake and were designed to dissipate forces before they destroy larger pieces of the bridge. The fasteners can be easily replaced with closing the bridge or stopping traffic. In 2004, UCSD structural engineering faculty members Seible and Chia-Ming Uang and alumnus Cole McDaniel were honored by the American Society of Civil Engineering with the Leon S. Moisseiff Award for the research that led to the design of these "fuse" fasteners. The new Bay Bridge span is scheduled to open in 2013. It will be a wonder of engineering: an 1,860-foot stretch of roadway suspended from a single tower, certifiably earthquake safe thanks to testing at UCSD. Powell Lab also tested elements for the Bay Area's new Carquinez and Benicia-Martinez Bridges.

Powell Lab also tests innovative prefabricated sections for bridges and roads. Old methods of construction using cast-in-place concrete are costly and dangerous, and it is a difficult process to pour large sections of concrete in and above huge bodies of water or deep canyons. By contrast, precast sections can be manufactured elsewhere, transported to the site, lowered into place by cranes or helicopters, and fastened together. Precast pieces had already been used around the world, but not in earthquake-prone zones. Prior to Powell Lab, there was no facility large enough to test such large structural elements in earthquake conditions.

The Big One is not a matter of *whether*, but *when*, as is true of earthquake prediction in seismically active regions around the world. Earthquake research conducted at Powell Lab will ensure safer structures as California continues to grow, saving many lives.

When Bruce Nauman was invited by the Stuart Collection to create a work at UCSD, he initially wanted to post his neon words atop La Jolla Playhouse's Mandell Weiss Theatre, where they would be visible to thousands of motorists each day. Neighbors did not take to that idea, which worked out well, since the Powell Structures Lab seems made for *Vices and Virtues.*

Nauman spelled out seven vices and seven virtues in seven-foot-high neon letters, with virtues in regular type and vices in italics. As overlapping neon letters flash on and off, vices and virtues run opposite directions around the top of the building, sometimes meeting up with each other: FAITH/LUST, HOPE/ENVY, CHARITY/SLOTH, PRUDENCE/PRIDE, JUSTICE/AVARICE, TEMPERANCE/GLUTTONY, AND FORTITUDE/ANGER.

Nauman used fourteen colors. Each letter combines two colors. There are eighty-eight letters, almost a mile of neon tubing. At night, Powell Lab becomes the campus's most visible public artwork, as artist Bruce Nauman's *Vices and Virtues* circles the top of the building.

Although the location of Nauman's work seems a stroke of fate, there is something cosmic about these simple good/evil sets of words in gigantic letters being associated with a building where what happens inside (testing structural elements) can make the difference between life and death.

12. High Bay Physics Laboratory
Liebhardt Weston and Associates, 1990

The third member of the three-building cluster of structural-testing facilities in this area of campus, the High Bay Physics Lab has been outfitted in recent years to test seismic response modification devices, or SRMDs. After major earthquakes in California during the eighties and nineties, Caltrans was eager to speed the invention of new materials and components for bridges and roads. Installed primarily for Caltrans, the building's testing equipment features a twelve-by-sixteen-foot testing table that moves over four low-friction bearings attached to the concrete floor. Forceful "actuators" jolt the platform back and forth to simulate a quake. Among the items tested here are dampers and isolator bearings.

Earthquake forces are not the only conditions simulated here. The aerospace industry is always on the lookout for lighter, stronger materials. One challenge in testing them is that their strengths and structural failures are more complex than the behavior of concrete and steel during earthquakes. In 2009, for the first time, UCSD engineers performed FAA-supervised tests of new carbon-fiber landing-gear components for a new Boeing aircraft. Utilizing the lab's large testing table, which can rotate as well as move horizontally and vertically, the components were subject to loads approaching one million pounds.

Architects Liebhardt and Weston are dedicated modernists whose spare, practical approach suited this project. Their preferences run to simple concrete-and-steel buildings, or wood post-and-beam buildings. Designing a single-purpose building for a practical and important purpose proved to be an ideal assignment. The large, boxy building, with its orderly arrays of concrete panels, reddish trim, and high row of windows, cuts an attractive profile that prevents it from looking out of place in this urban district.

13. Center for Magnetic Recording Research

Leonard Veitzer, 1986

The three-story building contains laboratories, academic and administrative offices, a lecture hall, conference room, and library. With its solid concrete-block forms, it resembles a heavy transformer like the ones used in audio amplifiers. The concrete has a practical purpose as well: preventing interference from outside communications.

The building is configured in a U-shape around a landscaped courtyard with plants that flower in spring, shade trees, and ferns that add lacy forms in front of the smooth concrete. Glass block walls at the entry bring daylight into the offices. All around the building, pockets of landscaping soften flat walls and recesses. Horizontal banks of windows are shaded by horizontal metal awnings that run the length of the building.

The center was founded in 1983 by a consortium of U.S. companies in the recording industry to research magnetic storage. Today, the center's mission is "to excel in research, education, and the transfer of innovative ideas in the field of information storage technology and systems." Researchers here collaborate with faculty from the departments of Mechanical and Aerospace Engineering, Electrical and Computer Engineering, NanoEngineering, and Physics.

Among the problems the Center for Magnetic Recording Research works on is how to keep hard drives from overheating as they become smaller and more densely packed with information, and how to pack more information onto flash memory cards. Technologies researched here also include error detection and correction and secure erasure.

Past and present sponsors of the CMRR include Ampex, Apple, Eastman Kodak, Fujitsu, Hewlett-Packard, IBM, Iomega, Lucent Technologies, Seagate, and Toshiba.

Center for Magnetic Recording Research

WALK EIGHT: UNIVERSITY CENTER AND SIXTH COLLEGE

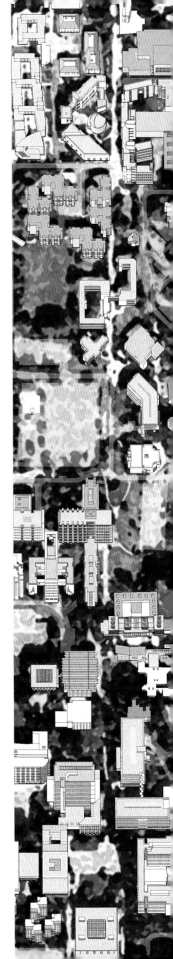

1. Geisel Library

William L. Pereira Associates, 1970

Addition

Gunnar Birkerts Associates and Buss, Silvers, Hughes & Associates, 1993

Early in the morning, wisps of fog often wrap the Geisel Library, adding mystery to its unusual jewel-like shape. Moving toward the building along Library Walk, one sees a shadowy form that gradually becomes more defined. Stepped forms and curves take shape, and the building begins its daily academic ritual as crowds stream through the doors. Geisel Library is the symbolic and cosmic center of campus intellectual life.

Generations of visitors have noted the eight-story, 110-foot-tall library's surreal identity: it is a spaceship or a lantern, or a gigantic crystal, or maybe an exotic structure left by an alien life form. Indeed, the building is at least partly rooted in science fiction. Architect William Pereira was fond of sci-fi novels, sleek cars, cities of the future, and other fantastic ideas that first captivated him when, in his first job out of architecture school at the University of Illinois, he helped plan the 1933 Chicago World's Fair with the theme "A Century of Progress."

When he was hired to design UCSD's library, Pereira's credits already included the Disneyland Hotel (1955), the spiderlike Theme Building (1961) at Los Angeles International Airport, and an Academy Award for the special effects on the film *Reap the Wild Wind* (1942). Pereira also designed San Francisco's signature tower, the forty-eight-story Transamerica Pyramid (1972).

Pereira's office was in Los Angeles, and his interest in science fiction coincided with the careers of authors such as Ray Bradbury, whose novel *Fahrenheit 451*, published in 1953, depicted a frightening future where books are confiscated and burned. Bradbury pounded out *Fahrenheit* on a 10-cents-an-hour typewriter in the UCLA library. In a direct connection between the author's wild imagination and the design of buildings, Bradbury served as a consultant to the Jerde Partnership during its design of downtown San Diego's fantastical Horton Plaza Shopping Center.

Geisel Library was the pet project of Chancellor John S. Galbraith, who accepted the job of chancellor only after he was promised that the university would build a major library. Galbraith believed that a university was only as good as its book collection, and he advocated Pereira's provocative design for the campus's largest and most important building. Today, as UCSD's flagship building, the Geisel Library houses four of UCSD's nine libraries.

Rising from a dramatic canyon site, the library is both a bold architectural statement and a sensitive response to the environment: large glass panels connect interior spaces with the outdoors through views of blue sky, shifting clouds, and eucalyptus

Geisel Library

trees that waver in the wind. Cantilevered from a concrete stalk, the library is framed in structural concrete that allows wide-open floors uncluttered by columns and walls.

Cradled like a precious stone, the main steel-and-glass library structure is supported by sixteen cast-in-place angled concrete columns (or "bents"), four on each side. The concrete carries a horizontal wood grain left by the wood forms used for casting. The building utilized 38,000 square feet of glass and 17,000 cubic yards of concrete.

Even before the Central Library opened, the buzz around the building was already helping to build the university's identity as a place of serious education and research. The collection has become one of the finest in Southern California. The UCSD libraries now hold more than seven million print and digital volumes and other materials in their collection. Special collections range from early California diaries to Theodor "Dr. Seuss" Geisel's sketches, interviews, commercial graphic designs, and other fascinating items. In 1995, the Central Library was renamed in Geisel's honor, following the $20 million gift bestowed by his widow, Audrey. His personal literacy crusade included the popular children's book *The Cat in the Hat* (1957), which incorporated 236 essential words for children suggested by his publisher.

Over time, as Pereira's design became known around the world, it was adapted as the university's official logo—one of the earliest examples of the power of architecture

to create an institution's identity. In 1992, the library was renovated and the floor plan, which had been altered with interior walls over the years, was restored to a more open configuration similar to Pereira's original plan.

As UCSD outgrew Pereira's building, architect Gunnar Birkerts was hired to design an addition. Underground levels doubled the library's capacity without obscuring Pereira's architecture. The expanded library has room for 1.3 million books and contains 1,400 study cubicles. Where Pereira's iconic, sci-fi design aims for the stars, Birkerts reached for daylight from underground. The addition's sloped roofs are covered with a landscape of drought-tolerant plants. About the only signs of the expansion visible from the outside are five sawtooth glass skylights in the landscape around the base of the library. The skylights are positioned to bring daylight to the addition's three underground wings. Glass-enclosed stairwells lead to the new underground spaces, which look out on below-grade gardens landscaped with gravel and desert succulents. Study tables and desks look out on these gardens. Harsh fluorescent light tubes have been replaced with newer energy-conserving tubes that produce softer, more natural light. The subterranean spaces are just as open and light-filled as the original building. As UCSD continues to grow, and to outgrow buildings, Birkerts's building provides an example of how a major amount of new space can be added with minimal impact.

Of course, a building this cool is very appealing to Hollywood. It landed a cameo role as a laboratory in the film *Killer Tomatoes Strike Back!* (1990), and it served as the backdrop in a television ad for Nissan Automobiles, among other appearances.

From the day it opened, the Geisel Library has inspired legions of visitors, including many who never venture inside. They come just to marvel at the building's exotic appearance. Professor Alain Cohen joined UCSD's literature faculty in 1968. He recalls standing next to Pereira at the library's dedication ceremony: "He explained how we should experience the building. Lean back against the foundation and look up along one of the diagonal concrete columns, and project yourself into the sky of knowledge!"[1]

2. *Snake Path*
Alexis Smith, 1992

Step away from the library and onto the back of a 560-foot serpent slithering down the slope to the east. One's feet slide over hexagonal "scales" of colored slate, from the bifurcated tongue and red eyes, along the body, around a "Garden of Eden" with "forbidden" fruit trees including pomegranate, to the tail that coils around an existing concrete path. A marble bench is inscribed with a quote from eighteenth-century British poet Thomas Gray's "Ode on a Distant Prospect of Eton College" (1875):

Snake Path

Yet ah! why should they know their fate?

Since sorrow never comes too late

And happiness too swiftly flies

Thought would destroy their Paradise

No more; where ignorance is bliss

'Tis folly to be wise.

Farther down the path, a monumental book of reddish granite is engraved with words from Milton's *Paradise Lost* (1667): "And wilt thou not be loath to leave this Paradise, but shalt possess a Paradise within, happier far."

When Smith was selected by the Stuart Collection to create a piece at UCSD, she toured the campus and chose this highly visible site next to the campus's best-known building, the Geisel Library, a source of knowledge. (Smith based her work on the biblical story of the beginning of human awareness.) *Snake Path* consists of the path itself as well as a native landscape alongside it. While responding to the architectural and natural contexts, Smith also faced the technical challenge of install-ing a long, twisting garden on a steep hillside. Landscape architects Spurlock Poirier joined a team of soils experts, structural engineers, and subcontractors who worked closely with Smith.

Spurlock and Poirier often collaborate with artists. They worked with Jackie Ferrara on UCSD's *Terrace* and with Robert Irwin on the spectacular Central Garden at the Getty Center in Los Angeles. Like Smith's *Snake Path*, Irwin's garden occu-pies a steep slope and winding trail. Both projects required similar creativity from Spurlock and Poirier, who merged artistic ideas with practical considerations of landscape design and maintenance.

With its epic scale, striking design, and biblical and literary references, *Snake Path* provokes a variety of responses. Many visitors simply linger to absorb images, ideas, and emotions. Undergrads find resonance with their literary studies. In 2008, a Christian group protested the piece's alleged glorification of evil by standing on the snake's head and reciting prayers.

3. Library Walk
Peter Walker William Johnson & Partners, 1995

On warm spring days, crowds cluster around booths that run the length of this broad pedestrian promenade, offering everything from Thai chicken and religious and politi-cal brochures to tie-dyed T-shirts. Stretching south from Geisel Library through the heart of campus to the School of Medicine, Library Walk gives the campus a Main Street that provides visual and psychological orientation.

The idea of a grand promenade through the center of campus appeared in the first campus master plan by Robert Alexander and remained through successive

Library Walk

revisions of the plan. A new 1989 master plan by Skidmore, Owings & Merrill played up Library Walk as a bold stroke that would unify a scattered campus.

Bands of dark and light concrete create a signature striped pattern that provides a sense of place. Benches, bicycle racks, container plants, and intimate seating give human scale. The edge of Library Walk features elevated square concrete platforms, each of which bears the year of a graduating class. These emblems remind students that they are part of a special group, and that their class too will be commemorated here.

Library Walk was a major construction project, but it also preserves and emphasizes the campus's distinctive eucalyptus grove. Although this long concrete spine is the most visible feature of campus planning, the dense eucalyptus grove that runs alongside it is an equally vital feature. The hard-edged Library Walk and feathery eucalyptus grove draw our attention to a long border between the natural and the manmade.

Landscape architect Peter Walker studied landscape architecture at UC Berkeley at the same time as San Diego landscape architect Joseph Yamada, who helped draft UCSD's first campus master plan. Like Yamada, Walker's mentors included San Francisco Bay Area landscape architects Garrett Eckbo, Lawrence Halprin, and Thomas Church. From them, Walker learned the power of planning and landscape design to tie buildings together and create a series of intriguing experiences. Walker also learned to revere Mother Nature, and to utilize a site's strong natural features as part of a development plan.

He helped invent the idea that public art need not be limited to sculptures in strategic locations. In downtown San Diego, his Linear Park (now Martin Luther King Promenade) along Harbor Drive demonstrated how planning and landscape elements can become art through unconventional combinations of hardscape and plant materials, colors, and forms, such as the Linear Park's dark/light bands of concrete, which reference the Mexican shawls known as *serapes*.

Walker's Library Walk is a simple, elegant design that helps unify a campus that grew in fits and starts during the early years. Walker has described Library Walk as the university's "front porch." In truth, it is the expanded version of the ancient town square, where citizens gathered to swap ideas, buy and sell various wares, and reconnect with the place they call home.

4. Student Health Center
Tucker, Sadler & Bennett, 1974
Langdon Wilson, addition, 2003

Covered with narrow strips of pale brown wood siding, the one-story Student Health Center blends into the surrounding eucalyptus grove. The building consists of rectangular wings connected by a skylight with entrances on both ends through large glass doors–standing inside the lobby feels much like standing outside in the grove.

The eucalyptus trees and a carpet of their fallen leaves serve as the primary landscape. The edges of the building are lined with vertical trellises made from narrow strips of wood. The trellises provide privacy for examination rooms while admitting daylight.

It is possible to pass the Student Health Center without noticing it. The building is situated along busy Library Walk, just south of the spectacular Geisel Library and east of the colorful Price Center. Both are examples of flamboyant architecture intended to create a buzz. This building, on the other hand, is all about providing a pleasant (even inspiring) experience for its users while celebrating the eucalyptus grove that has become UCSD's signature landscape feature.

5. *Two Running Violet V Forms*
Robert Irwin, 1983

Angling through a eucalyptus grove at the heart of the campus, Robert Irwin's long bluish chain-link fence manipulates one's perceptions of light, form, color, and distance. In certain light, the raised fence is a mysterious ghostly presence. The more one looks at the fence, the more one notices the eucalyptus grove's variations of light and color. As one wanders through the grove, the high chain-link panels separate,

TOP: *Student Health Center*
BOTTOM: Two Running Violet V Forms

define, connect, distort, and blend forms and textures in the grove, causing fresh perceptions of the fence, the grove, the carpet of mottled dead leaves, and the changing light and sky. Depending on the weather, the season, and the time of day, Irwin's piece stands out in stark relief, or blends with the grove's green, gray, and violet shades. It sometimes disappears and re-emerges and blends in again as the viewer scans its length.

Irwin began his career as an abstract expressionist painter in fifties Los Angeles. In the seventies and eighties, he shifted to making installations that employed sheer white fabric to create ethereal, illusory environments that distorted one's perceptions of space and light. In that spirit, his *Two Running Violet V Forms* is more about the effects of the piece than about the form of the piece alone.

Wandering through the eucalyptus grove and experiencing Irwin's fence can be a transformative experience or an amusing one or both. The play of light and shadow reveals the mysterious—some might say spiritual—powers of nature. Some visitors arrive at other, more lighthearted interpretations: it is a big badminton net, or a bird-catcher. It has been the object of various pranks. Early one morning, visitors discovered a large papier-mâché bird lodged beak-first in the violet fence. But Irwin must be pleased that his net also captures bigger, human game, as is evident in the groups that gather to gaze at his work.

Career Services Center

6. Career Services Center
Martinez/Wong & Associates, 1985

Squares and circles are simple forms, yet this building shows how they can be combined so that their sum is greater than its parts. The architects use square white tiles, concrete, and reflective glass to create a variety of angular and cylindrical forms. The forms come alive with reflections in the glass of sky, clouds, trees, and people.

Students come here for career guidance. They meet with counselors, take advantage of assessments and career workshops, and find out which companies will be recruiting on campus. The building provides a friendly environment for both career guidance and administrative meetings in rooms like the circular conference chamber, with its round table that looks out on the grove.

Minimalist in forms and materials, the Career Services Center is a stark white contrast to the glitzy postmodern buildings of its era (such as architect Michael Graves's Aventine hotel/office project just across Interstate 5). This center offers a fresh take on the white modernist buildings of the German Bauhaus movement of the 1920s and its many American offspring in twentieth-century modern architecture.

With its strong shapes and hard edges, the building stands out from its setting in a eucalyptus grove—a different approach from campus buildings that blend with their natural settings. Even so, it also makes strong connections to the outdoors with sky-lights and large windows.

One measure of a building is how well it ages. This one has matured gracefully. The atrium reception area was expanded in 2008, and its elegant wood and muted palette of gray, green, and plum give the building a fresh, contemporary vibe.

7. International Center
UCSD architects and engineers, Robert Thorburn, Judith Munk, 1971

Nestled in a eucalyptus grove and set back from Library Walk, the International Center is a complex of modest buildings that serves as a calm oasis amid a busy and growing campus. Occupied by religious and student organizations and a day-care center, the buildings are arranged around a courtyard and covered open-air walkways.

UCSD architect Robert Thorburn collaborated on the building's design with designer Judith Munk, wife of famed Scripps Institution of Oceanography scientist Walter Munk. Judith Munk earned an architecture degree at Bennington College in Vermont, and worked for Richard Neutra in Los Angeles.

TOP: *International Center*

BOTTOM: *Center Hall*

The International Center's buildings are sited to create courtyards, gardens, and walkways that connect it with nearby paths. Surrounding eucalyptus trees add to a parklike effect. A tree-shaded deck on the east side is the kind of place one expects to find at a rustic mountain lodge.

8. Center Hall
NBBJ, 1996

Like a hinge for human movement, the open rotunda at the corner of Center Hall connects the building to Library Walk and guides pedestrians around or into the building. Center Hall is situated at the midpoint of Library Walk, the wide pedestrian mall that runs south from Geisel Library. This location is a busy intersection for various paths across campus, and Center Hall creates a focal public place.

Center Hall is an elegantly appointed building of classical proportions, with clearly defined ground, middle, and upper levels. It is crowned by a slanted green roof supported by large wood beams. The use of concrete on the first floor gives it a heavy, grounded effect. Smooth pastel-hued stucco makes the second level lighter, more buoyant. The third level is mostly glass, which reflects the changing panorama of sky, clouds, and trees.

The building contains computer labs, teacher training labs, meeting rooms, and classrooms used by various departments. All around the building are intimate outdoor spaces, including a quiet tree-shaded garden in back, small courtyards, and second- and third-level balconies and walkways with bird's-eye views.

The rotunda's importance is reinforced with concrete-block towers on either side of the entryway. Steel staircases rise diagonally inside the rotunda, where the movement of people is as colorful and dynamic as at a busy subway station. The people-friendly design approach continues along the building's edges, which are punctuated by broad steps, covered arcades, and small groupings of concrete benches.

Several large white concrete balls rest in front of the main entry, as though they rolled to a stop here. Students plop down for cell phone sessions or coffee breaks supplied by the espresso cart tucked in Center Hall's rotunda. Several more balls rest in the garden behind the building: one imagines they may have rolled in the night through the rotunda and out the other side. The balls are not part of UCSD's Stuart Collection of public art, which had lobbied for their removal since they were not approved by the Stuart Collection and its highly regarded curators. But students rallied successfully to save their balls.

Seattle-based NBBJ Architects is one of the largest architecture companies in the world, with projects ranging from academic to medical buildings and significant public spaces. NBBJ has also designed buildings at UC Berkeley and UCLA.

In Center Hall NBBJ addressed some of the same challenges it faced a decade later with the design of Atkinson Hall engineering building, with its wide range of programmatic requirements and the need for high visibility. Center Hall solved the problem of knitting a major building into a complex public space.

9. University Center 107 (Chancellor's Complex)
Russell Forester, 1964

Cubic forms in narrow wood siding give this complex a look that one might describe as "rustic modernism." Symmetrical groupings of windows let in plenty of daylight. The windows are shaded by awnings made of narrow strips of wood. Large sliding glass doors open onto the central landscaped courtyard, with its overhanging shade trees, or to open-air arcades under flat roofs supported by wood columns and beams.

Eleven low buildings stretch between the Price Center on the north and Center Hall on the south. University Center 107's main entrance is on the north side, where it is set back from a wide pedestrian street and screened by a landscape of street trees, narrow lawns, and a stone garden wall of rough-hewn stones.

By the seventies, architect Russell Forester had mostly switched his focus from architecture to painting, in a minimalist abstract style that incorporated basic geometric forms. Buildings by Forester such as this one exhibit that same fascination with expressing himself in as few simple forms as possible.

University Center 107

While most other campus departments and offices have long since moved from their original quarters to larger, more flamboyant buildings, the office of the university's most powerful executive, the chancellor, remains here in modest buildings that create an unintimidating environment. Even the greenest frosh can visit the chancellor's office without the anxiety he or she might feel when visiting a faculty member or university administrator in some of campus's large, minimalist concrete buildings.

10. Student Services Center
Rob Wellington Quigley Architects, 2007

Rob Wellington Quigley's five-story Student Services Center combines the neighborhood's predominant concrete, steel, and glass in a spirited building that ties in with its context. The center combines essential student services in one convenient location: Registrar's, Financial Aid, Graduate Studies, and Admissions offices, and the Triton Center, where families and prospective students begin their campus visits. The building also includes meeting and conference rooms and a three-hundred-seat auditorium equipped with giant roll-up doors that connect its lobby with the parklike landscape.

Student Services is a centerpiece of UCSD's emerging urban center, where mixed-use designs create a neighborhood that is busy all day. UCSD needed a prominent center. With a population on the order of forty thousand, it is a small city unto itself. To serve the campus community, the building also includes a copy shop, a frozen-yogurt outlet, and a restaurant.

Elevated above pedestrian arcades, the building allows easy movement through its base. Tall glass around the first floor lets visitors look inside and employees see out, encouraging human interaction. Balconies and outdoor walkways connect offices and conference rooms on upper levels. Terraces, stairs, decks, and landings overlook the landscape.

The building is configured in an L-shape that wraps Matthews Quad, with its expansive lawn. Near the building, wavy sculptural benches look like public art but they are also comfortable places to kick back with a book. The quad is landscaped with indigenous Torrey pines and California sycamores, as well as Canary Island date palms and Monterey cypresses that remain from Camp Matthews, the military rifle range that once occupied the site. A Star pine anchors the center's southeast corner; a cedar tree, the northwest.

The Town Square to the west of Student Services is a wide public space where a farmers market offers fresh produce. Simply landscaped with a lawn and pine and black acacia trees, the square includes the original Camp Matthews flagpole and a granite monument commemorating the old World War II military base.

Artist Michael Asher's *Untitled* (1991), commissioned by the Stuart Collection, is situated at the north end of the Square (formerly the site of the headquarters for

Student Services Center

Camp Matthews military base). Rather than create a conspicuous installation, Asher added a granite drinking fountain replicating fountains in offices and government buildings. By placing a subtly decorated fountain in an outdoor park, Asher asks the viewer to reconsider what constitutes art. Asher's everyday fountain becomes a public work of art by nature of its placement in context with the military commemorative stone and the United States flag.

Quigley has broad experience designing public buildings and spaces. His credits include the Children's Museum in downtown San Diego, San Diego's new main library (on hold for budgetary reasons), numerous branch libraries, and award-winning transit centers in Escondido and Solana Beach. His projects also include master plans in San Diego neighborhoods such as Ocean Beach, Vista, and Imperial Beach. All of this experience came together with the Student Services Center, in which countless successful design details have been utilized.

When he began his career in the eighties, Quigley was among the first San Diego architects to incorporate elements such as passive solar and generous daylighting to cut energy consumption. He is also a pioneer in the use of recycled materials, such as the recycled-plastic-bag lumber, restroom tiles of recycled glass, and countertops of recycled plastic adopted in the center.

For its "inviting nature...openness...and unexpected playful details," the building won an Honor Award—the highest recognition—from the San Diego chapter of the American Institute of Architects in 2007.

The Conrad Prebys Music Center

11. Conrad Prebys Music Center
LMN Architects and Cyril Harris, 2009

Soon after the Department of Music occupied Mandeville Center in 1975, composers and performers realized that this general-use performance facility was not ideal for music. They began to imagine a new center dedicated to the range of music studied, composed, and performed at UCSD. After more than twenty years of planning, the three-story Conrad Prebys Music Center finally provides those spaces. The 400-seat Conrad Prebys Concert Hall is the building's centerpiece. Designed by renowned acoustician Cyril Harris and architect Mark Reddington of LMN Architects, it is considered one of the finest small concert halls in the world.

To isolate the hall from outside noise, it is designed as a separate room within the building's thick concrete outer walls, with soundproofing in between the walls. The ceiling is suspended from spring-loaded cables that dampen outside vibrations. Heating and cooling equipment is silent.

The acoustical ceiling and wall system is an asymmetrical shell of bamboo panels, angled to diffuse sound evenly through the hall. As a result, live music seems to bloom from the stage, engulfing listeners in every seat.

The Gala Opening Concert in May 2009 caused a buzz in the media and in the music community with premieres of experimental pieces by UCSD composers Rand Steiger, Lei Liang, Anthony Davis, and Roger Reynolds. The following month, the department's Camera Lucida chamber music series introduced classical music lovers to the hall's excellent acoustics.

The concrete, steel, and glass music center also contains an experimental theater with an electronic Meyer Sound system that emulates sonic environments ranging from flat (with no echo or sense of spaciousness) to the kind of echo you might hear if you yelled into a canyon. Nearby is a 150-seat lecture/recital hall. Elsewhere are an orchestral rehearsal room, a state-of-the-art recording studio, computer labs, rehearsal rooms, and, in a corner suite on the first floor, the headquarters for the percussion program directed by renowned percussionist Steven Schick. Skylights, light wells, and plenty of windows bring natural light to many rooms and hallways.

The music center was designed to fit with surrounding buildings in the urban district. A landscape of bamboo, flowering shrubs, and a variety of drought-tolerant greenery softens the angles and stark surfaces. Along Russell Lane, across from Gilman Parking Structure, the center beckons visitors with a wide entry and court-yard that accommodates receptions and concerts. At the music center's dedication, following a speech by Chancellor Marye Anne Fox, UCSD's gospel choir filled the courtyard with hundreds of soaring voices.

At the building's northeast corner, transparent glass lets visitors watch musi-cians rehearsing in the experimental theater. Outside the concert hall, at the build-ing's northwest corner, huge glass doors slide open so that the lobby and courtyard become one large reception area.

The music center's completion marked a milestone for UCSD and for San Diego. At a university famous for the sciences and research, the new music center validates the arts as an essential part of education.

12. Gilman Parking Structure
Rob Wellington Quigley, 2002

In any development project, parking is a high priority. In recent years, architects have

discovered ways to design parking structures that are more attractive than the ones some of us remember from the sixties and seventies. San Diego architect Rob Quigley has built his career around unusual designs for common building types, such as libraries, churches, transit stations—and parking lots.

Gilman Parking Structure

At the busy southeast entrance to campus, Gilman Parking Structure is a dynamic design in exposed concrete. The building combines several levels of parking with offices for UCSD parking services and a credit union. When pedestrians passing by outside look at this building, simple design details conceal the fact that it is a big box full of cars. Rows of cars are concealed by cable railings, translucent panels, and strips of perforated aluminum assembled like strands of a woven basket. Stone tiles add elegance to the busy elevator towers.

Solar panels atop the structure exemplify UCSD's commitment to green power. Steel trees support the solar arrays, angled toward the sun like giant flowers on the prowl for photosynthesis. The panels produce 275,000 kilowatts of power annually, enough to power ten houses. Every year, the array prevents 263,480 pounds of carbon dioxide emissions and displaces 155,980 pounds of coal.

By locating major parking structures around the edge of campus, planners can reserve the center of campus for pedestrians. And the places where there are no cars on campus become parklike locations ideal for walking and thinking and socializing and learning and creating.

13. Sixth College Apartments

Alfredo Araiza and Associates, 1980
Rosen and Jones, 1984

(Note: Although these buildings are a part of Sixth College, they are included in the University Center chapter because they make a convenient stop on your University Center walking tour.)

Public spaces and landscaping unify two apartment complexes built within four years of each other at UCSD's Sixth College.

Alfredo Araiza and Associates' Matthews Apartments consist of five two-story buildings, each with eight apartments, a study hall, and two student lounges.

Buildings in the Matthews complex are tan stucco with brown wood trim and railings. First-floor patios and second-level balconies line the landscape in a parklike landscape of lawn, mature trees such as carob and cottonwood, and flowering shrubs including guavas that bear edible fruit.

Sixth College Apartments

Next door, Rosen and Jones's Sixth College Apartments include two- to four-bedroom apartments in eighteen three-story buildings and utilize a similar palette of tan stucco and brown wood trim, but with steeper roofs and angular wood trellises, roof beams, and deep eaves that give the complex a hint of Swiss chalet. The landscape is also similar, but with different species of trees including pine and coral.

A plaza along the seam between the two complexes brings the neighborhood together. Tables, benches, and elevated concrete planters provide plenty of seating, and umbrellas and mature trees add plenty of shade. The two complexes share a "community lodge" for various special events. This residential enclave of low stucco buildings and lush landscaping feels like a typical Southern California suburb. It even has a tree-lined street.

The green, serene environment gives students a place to escape from the hectic urban center of campus only a few blocks away. These apartments are extremely popular with students—and with their parents, who are impressed with an inviting neighborhood quite different from the high-rise student dorms where many of them spent some undergrad years.

14. Pepper Canyon Hall
SmithGroup, 2005

Reflecting UCSD's pedestrian-friendly plan for the campus's urban center, the four-story Pepper Canyon Hall is so open and inviting that once you enter the courtyard, you almost forget there is a building surrounding you. The building's universal appeal is suited to its role as a flexible building, used as temporary space by rapidly expanding departments until their permanent buildings are completed.

With the university projecting 35 percent enrollment growth between 2002 and 2010, Pepper Canyon Hall was fast-tracked and completed in two years. It is made of glass, steel, concrete, and brick—familiar materials on campus. SmithGroup's design incorporates several smart features: subtle integration of structural elements and landscape; narrow horizontal openings in the front facade to give the building a light, transparent appearance; balconies and stairs to provide outdoor circulation.

The courtyard is a pleasant place to spend time, on benches shaded by deciduous Tipu trees that come alive in spring with dense green canopies and tiny yellow blossoms. In the courtyard, a narrow elevated bed is planted with a row of spiky green shoots against a concrete wall. Concrete planters line the edge of the main staircase.

Pepper Canyon Hall sits across Russell Lane from the Conrad Prebys Music Center, just south of the Visual Arts Building and around the corner from the Student Services Center. Like Pepper Canyon Hall, these neighboring buildings are all open

TOP: *Pepper Canyon Hall*
BOTTOM: *Visual Arts Facility*

and inviting at street level. Broad public entrances encourage an easy flow of people in and out of the building. Transparent glass at the street level engages pedestrians with people and activity inside the building.

Pepper Canyon's thoughtful design and smart integration with the campus plan earned a Citation Award in 2005 from the Los Angeles chapter of the American Institute of Architects, as well as an Honor Award from San Diego's AIA chapter in 2007.

15. Visual Arts Facility

Neptune Thomas Davis and Rebecca Binder, 1993

Technically a part of Sixth College (UCSD's newest college, not yet formally named), the Visual Arts Facility (VAF) is a vital piece of University Center. Along the northern end of Russell Lane, the VAF consists of five interconnected pavilions, arranged around courtyards.

The Department of Visual Arts faculty includes (or has included) internationally renowned artists such as painter and former film critic Manny Farber, multimedia artist Adriene Jenik, visual/computer artist Sheldon Brown, and sculptor Jennifer Pastor. In the ongoing recruitment of top faculty and graduate students, design architect Rebecca Binder's building has proven to be a significant recruitment tool. Visiting artists are impressed with the twenty-four faculty studios, fifty-one studios for graduate students, performance and gallery spaces, workshops, TV studios, media and editing suites, and communications and seminar spaces.

Creating art is an introspective process, but it can also involve heavy labor and require large working areas—such as the space provided by the VAF's courtyards. The VAF is a durable building with an industrial aesthetic of exposed ducts, vents, pipes, and steel framing. Wood, steel, and concrete provide raw surfaces for interesting forms. Walls, railings, stairs, and roofs come together to create surprising angles and forms that produce changing patterns of light and shadow.

Away from its urban edge on Russell Lane, the VAF backs onto a eucalyptus grove crossed by dirt trails. Large, sweet-scented trees shelter a quiet outdoor area where artists can take a break from their intensive work.

Binder's architecture (Neptune Thomas served as production architects, producing detailed construction drawings) is rooted in sharp modernism as well as the wilder, experimental architecture of contemporary Southern California. She earned an MA in architecture from UCLA in 1975 and has taught at the Southern California Institute of Architecture (SCI-Arc), a hothouse of an architectural school that grew some of California's most innovative architects of Binder's generation. Binder's VAF brings together the best ideas from her formative years: modernism's functionalism and honest use of materials, as well as edgier elements like her off-kilter site plan and unpredictably slanted roofs.

16. Science and Engineering Research Facility

MBT Architecture, 1996

Featuring a pedestrian-friendly perimeter with an open arcade, the Science and Engineering Research Facility (SERF) brings activity to the wide pedestrian walk that runs past newer buildings also including the Price Center and the Student Services Center.

Science and Engineering Research Facility

SERF is the headquarters of UCSD's Department of Structural Engineering. It contains administrative and faculty offices as well as the Offices of Graduate and Undergraduate Studies. The back of SERF connects to the Powell Structural Components Lab, where hardware, materials, and structural components are earthquake-tested.

The four-story SERF building is proportioned to fit with neighboring buildings, with horizontal bands of concrete defining each floor. Exterior walls are clad in smooth-textured stucco and anodized aluminum paneling. Set back from the street behind a row of trees, the SERF building's arcade runs along the south and east sides. Wide wood benches in these covered pedestrian areas encourage people to linger in the fresh air. Awnings on the third and fourth floors shade interior spaces from sunlight (and excessive heat gain).

Like the neighboring Student Services Center, Price Student Center, and Visual Arts Facility, SERF is designed to reinforce UCSD's emerging urban center. With its elegant, carefully detailed design, this is another link in a chain of successful buildings that form a new campus center.

17. Price Center West

Kaplan/McLaughlin/Diaz and Austin/Hansen/ Fehlman, 1989

Bookstore Expansion

Cannon Design—Mehrdad Yazdani Studio, 2008

Borrowing its scale and mixed-use design from European streetscapes, the Price Center gives the campus a much-needed social hub. The building contains a bookstore, food court, copy center, offices, and meeting rooms. It is configured in a U shape around a multilevel courtyard. Since its opening in 1989, the building and courtyard have become the busiest places on campus.

The Price Center was among the first of a new generation of larger campus buildings built in the nineties, designed by prominent architects in more flamboyant style than buildings from the sixties and seventies. Here, bold forms are covered in greenish glass, rough off-white Jerusalem stone, and smoother yellowish Portuguese stone. Curves and circles—such as round windows and the curved glass wall above the plaza—are themes that unify the array of strong forms. Along with the bold architecture, the smart planning makes the center an inviting and lively place.

The plaza is terraced like an amphitheater, dotted with shade trees, and features a sea of umbrella-shaded tables. In the northwest corner, a theater marquee advertises films and other campus events. Terraces along the edges of the building, around the courtyard, are great perches for watching people in the plaza below. On sunny days—which are most days—the plaza comes alive around noon, when bands take a stage set up under the marquee. The crescendo of conversations at outdoor tables gets almost as loud as the music.

From Library Walk along the Price Center's open west side, a broad, grassy slope leads down to the plaza. The grassy slope is bordered by steps that run along the buildings edges down into the courtyard. Water spills down through terraced pools along the steps that enter the Price Center from the southwest corner.

Meanwhile, pedestrians approaching the Price Center from Warren Plaza at the northeast corner come into its courtyard through a broad outdoor opening. On the building's south side are entrances to the food court, coffeehouse, Price Center Ballroom, and the UCSD Bookstore.

When it opened, some criticized the building for its large scale and flamboyant forms and materials. It marked a departure from the campus's original rustic wood buildings and stark modernist towers. Some students protested the arrival of fast-food chain restaurants in the food court, but the service and quality of food have proven to be high. For those who prefer a different atmosphere, the old student center at Revelle College is a modest complex of wood buildings with a pub, coffeehouse, and used bookstore, so the campus accommodates a range of tastes and needs.

UCSD Bookstore is the campus's prime retail outlet, offering textbooks, mass-market books, magazines, electronics, UCSD sweatshirts and souvenirs, office supplies, birthday cards—even electric guitars. To better serve students and enhance the university's revenue stream, the Price Center bookstore addition included expansion space for the existing bookstore at Price Center. It also added a coffeehouse that serves some of the best espresso on campus. The expansion matches the forms and elegant stone-cladding of the original building and merges seamlessly with the original through new openings, steps, and hallways.

The expanded bookstore has a convenient new entrance along busy Library Walk, to the east of Price Center. On the north side, broad steps lead to the second-floor lobby outside the Price Center Ballroom. Wide openings on the first floor link the new cafe with the bookstore. The connection between the retail store and the coffee is good business for everyone: The longer people stay in the store, the more espresso they drink. The longer they linger with their coffee, the more likely they are to spend money in the store.

TOP: *Price Center East Expansion atrium with artist Barbara Kruger's installation* Another.
BOTTOM: *Price Center West*

Both the south and east additions were designed for energy efficiency. They both earned prestigious Silver certification from LEED in recognition of features such as low-wattage fluorescent lighting and reduced heating and cooling needs with the precise placement of windows to capture sunlight in winter and screen it out during summer.

18. Price Center East Expansion
Cannon Design—Mehrdad Yazdani Studio, 2008

Energized by a busy food court, an experimental performance venue, and artist Barbara Kruger's Stuart Collection installation *Another*, the Price Center East Expansion is a dynamic, high-tech counterpoint to the original building. Where the earlier Price Student Center building is covered with elegant stone in a variety of decorative patterns, the addition has an economical exterior of minimalist stucco and glass. Architect Mehrdad Yazdani of Cannon Design thinks of the addition as "two square tubes."

Price Center East Expansion

The sides of these long, narrow tubes are pierced by narrow windows that make the building look like a futuristic machine. Walls of glass cover the ends of the tubes, which allows natural light to flood the food court as well as the upper floors. Set in an atrium at the intersection of Yazdani's "tubes," the food court is a cafeteria with dozens of tables, surrounded by fast food restaurants around the atrium's perimeter.

The addition connects seamlessly to the original building. A bright yellow corridor links a food court in the old wing to the new one. On the second level, a wide hallway leads from the original building's lobby to a second-level lobby in the new wing, near the performance venue The Loft. Large display cases are built into walls along the connecting corridors; they are used by a variety of campus organizations and are sometimes full of art.

With is soaring height, crisscrossing upper levels, and industrial materials (concrete, steel, aluminum), the atrium in the East Addition, which houses the new food court, has the excitement of a concert hall or dramatic theater.

The atrium food court has a strong Wi-Fi signal, of course, and laptops are as common here as lunch trays. Free access to computer terminals is also available here. Small meeting rooms occupy one corner of the atrium, and there is a post office in another corner.

Since completion, the East Expansion has enhanced the popularity and convenience of the campus's busiest gathering place. As new freshmen arrive every fall, they soon flock to this busy urban area.

WALK NINE: UCSD SCHOOL OF MEDICINE

1. Stein Clinical Research Building
Arthur Erickson Associates, 1992

From a distance, the rotunda of the Sam and Rose Stein Clinical Research Building rises from a thicket of mature landscaping like a ghostly version of historical pavilions in the Beaux Arts parks of decades past. The sleek building is covered with gun-metal-gray aluminum panels and greenish glass. The four-story entry rotunda resembles a giant microscope or scientific testing device. It actually contains the building's elevators and the mechanical equipment that removes toxic fumes from laboratories.

The entry rotunda is the building's hub. It is flanked by three- and four-story wings. While access to the wings is limited due to the sensitive research taking place inside, the entry rotunda is pierced with multiple three-story openings that offer views from the front of the building through the rotunda to the parklike landscape behind the building. The building may be semi-private, but the outdoor area is an inviting public place used for graduations and other special occasions.

Flexible, open labs encourage interaction and camaraderie among researchers. Glass walls between labs and offices inside the wings place researchers within view of each other, enhancing their sense of a shared mission. Many offices have views of the campus and landscape.

Over the years, research in this building has included investigations into sleep patterns, HIV-AIDS, memory, and aging. The Stein Institute for Research on Aging brings together dozens of researchers from medicine, bioengineering, family and preventive medicine, orthopaedics, neuroscience, surgery, and psychiatry. They collaborate to explore the mechanisms of Alzheimer's disease, cancer, arthritis, osteoporosis, glaucoma, atherosclerosis, diabetes, and late-onset schizophrenia, among others.

Arthur Erickson was an internationally renowned Canadian architect whose projects ranged from the Museum of Glass in Tacoma, Washington, and the Donald Bruce Kaufman Library in Los Angeles, to the waterfront San Diego Convention Center, with its distinctive concrete buttresses lining Harbor Drive.

Today, with the campus trend toward open, pedestrian-friendly buildings, Erickson might not design such a prominent but intensely private structure. But the Stein Building's unusual design makes it a significant sculptural icon that signifies the vast mysteries and exciting frontiers of medical research.

2. Medical Teaching Facility
Mosher Drew Watson Ferguson, 1976

Bringing together two modes of seventies modernism (concrete brutalism and California's weathered-wood take on modernism), the Medical Teaching Facility

TOP: *Sam and Rose Stein Clinical Research Building*
BOTTOM: *Medical Teaching Facility*

combines a northern section of three stories in concrete and a two-story southern section covered in vertical wood siding. The concrete piece fits with other concrete-and-glass medical school buildings nearby. While the materials of the front and rear sections are different, their proportions and scale are similar, giving them a unified appearance. The sections are connected by concrete bridges that cross above a courtyard of mature trees. This courtyard between buildings flows into a second courtyard at the heart of the U-shaped south building.

Over the years, the back section's wood has weathered, forming organic patterns that tell of hot summers, wet winters, and morning mists. The rustic exterior suits the green landscape immediately to the south of the Medical Teaching Facility, with its lawns, eucalyptus trees, and shade trees.

The Medical Teaching Facility houses offices, classrooms, and research areas, including Radiation Medicine and the Lipid Analytic Lab, which explores the role of cellular fats and oils in heart disease, stroke, diabetes, and Alzheimer's disease.

Just south of the building, artist Kiki Smith's sculpture *Standing* (1988) rests on a broad green lawn cut by curvy concrete sidewalks. The piece consists of a bronze casting of a woman's body atop a casting of a tree trunk. The work is part of UCSD's Stuart Collection of public art. The tree's "bark" reveals the trails traced by insects on the bark of the campus's eucalyptus trees. Smith imagines that these lines are records of what may have caused the tree's death, and they also resemble veins and capillaries—essential to human life. A necklace of starfish-headed pins in the shape of the constellation Virgo pierces the woman's bodice, evoking images of acupuncture or dissection or martyrdom. Water runs like blood from the hands. As a symbol of Virgo, the necklace also represents the oceanic and the celestial, mind and body, flesh and healing.

3. Leichtag Biomedical Research Building
Zimmer Gunsul Frasca Partnership, 2003

When the new millennium opened, UCSD's School of Medicine had nearly doubled its requirement for research space since its founding in 1963. Thanks to a $12 million contribution from the Leichtag Family Foundation, the university hired prominent Oregon-based architects Zimmer Gunsul Frasca Partnership to design a building that is the jewel of the medical school. The Leichtag Foundation's mission is finding cures for childhood diseases, and that is a primary focus of the research in this building.

The building contains labs, support spaces, and offices. With its spectacular architecture, state-of-the-art facilities, and innovative research, the facility stimulates growth and funding for biomedical science. It is also an asset to the university's ongoing recruitment of faculty and grad-student researchers.

Occupying a prominent site along Gilman Drive, the Leichtag Building is clad in glass and rich polished stone. A full-height glass facade along Library Walk includes an entrance that leads to a five-story atrium lobby. Artist Ed Carpenter's seventy-two-foot-tall sculpture of stainless steel and glass (2004)—not a part of the Stuart Collection of public art—seems to float in the space. The piece is tethered to cables that run from the ceiling to a circle of benches designed by Carpenter on the atrium's first floor. The suspended sculpture hovers in front of balconies on four levels where benches provide views of the vertigo-inducing sculpture in the soaring atrium. With its steel beams and cables, the piece could be a section of one of the bridges the artist has designed in other cities.

Carpenter is fascinated with the ways in which his creations manipulate light, and this piece changes with the daylight that streams through the lobby windows. The towering sculpture also resembles minuscule forms that might be seen through a microscope. Carpenter hopes his piece provokes interaction and

Leichtag Family Foundation Biomedical Research Building

Leichtag Family Foundation Medical Research Building

discussion among scientists. After all, the atrium is formally referred to as the "Scholarly Interaction Space."

The building's long south side looks out on the medical school's central rolling lawn. The south side entrance is shaded by curved wood awnings resting atop concrete-and-steel "trees." A nearby espresso cart fuels the researchers. A broad terrace with shaded tables steps down to the plaza and provides views of several buildings that surround the plaza. South side balconies look down on the grassy open space behind the building. Translucent glass panels are mounted within steel-frame railings, so that the balconies do not feel boxed in.

Across the plaza, the Biomedical Library, with its tentlike roof, offers a study in contrasts between campus architecture circa 1969 and in the new millennium, its precast concrete panels and wavy concrete roof providing a counterpoint to the Leichtag building's more angular forms and sharply contrasting materials.

4. Biomedical Sciences Building
Robert Alexander, 1968

When the School of Medicine opened in 1968, the six-story Biomedical Sciences Building was the school's all-purpose headquarters. Over the years it has been a durable and versatile structure, changing to meet the demands of rapidly evolving technologies, research, and courses.

As a testament to the building's timeless appeal and a show of loyalty to tradition, the medical school's dean's office and administrative offices remain here today, even though newer and more spectacular buildings now surround it. The building also includes a variety of laboratories as well as the Liebow and Garren auditoriums, which accommodate frequent lectures, conferences, and symposiums.

Other important research spaces in the building include the Biomarker Core Facility (measuring biomarkers of inflammation and autoimmunity) to the Comparative Neuromuscular Lab (diagnostic testing of neuromuscular disorders affecting domestic animals).

Like early UCSD buildings at Muir and Revelle colleges, this building is a concrete-frame structure with an exterior of concrete and precast concrete panels. The panels feature recessed arches that march in horizontal rows across the exterior, interspersed with horizontal bands of concrete. The small arches serve a green function by channeling daylight into the building while screening out harsh direct sun that could overheat interior spaces.

The building connects with the Biomedical Library (also designed by Alexander) to form an L that defines the southeast corner of the plaza at the heart of the School of Medicine. Situated near the library's entrance, the entrance to Biomedical Sciences is defined by a low concrete arch over a covered walkway that leads to the entry doors. The concrete roof above the walkway is partially open to the sky between long, narrow concrete beams.

In recent years, the building has undergone numerous small renovations. In the basement, an old photo-processing lab became offices for various areas of research, including the Harasz Anatomy Lab. The lobby—the most visible space inside the building—was updated in 2002 with contemporary forms, materials, and colors. Original lobby doors were replaced with glass doors that brighten the space with daylight. A purple light soffit recessed into the ceiling sheds soft, uniform light into new flexible work areas. Original wood paneling remains as a reminder of the building's long, rich history.

Biomedical Sciences Building

In pictures of UCSD taken in the sixties, the campus is almost unrecognizable compared to how it looks today. Where once there were only low military buildings surrounded by hundreds of barren acres, now there are dozens of buildings amid mature landscaping. The university and medical school have grown up around the Basic Sciences Building, and it has aged gracefully. It looks just as interesting and innovative as it did the day it was dedicated. Today, though, the landscaping is lush and mature, and creeping vines crawl high up the walls, adding natural art to the concrete surfaces.

5. Biomedical Library
Robert Alexander, 1969

Biomedical Library Renovation and Expansion
Hardy Holzman Pfeiffer, 2006

A tentlike roof floats above the spacious reading room on the top floor of the Biomedical Library, where tables are almost always crowded with medical students. The 2006 expansion added a new reading room that connects with the original to create one spacious room that runs the full length of the combined second floor. The addition's roof captures some of the light, floating vibe of the original roof. Whereas the original is a series of peaks, like white tents in the Arabian desert, the new roof runs horizontal until it angles skyward at the building's south end.

The Biomedical Library is a vital resource for UCSD's clinicians, researchers, and students. As San Diego's only dedicated biomedical research library, it also serves the region's numerous biotechnology and life sciences enterprises, as well as physicians. It is also open to the public. The new complex combines architect Robert Alexander's three-level library (1969) with Hardy Holzman Pfeiffer's empathetic three-story addition (2006). The addition included renovating the old building, updating the interior and seamlessly connecting it to the new building. Entrances at the south (the addition) and the north (the original building) are connected by a new lobby.

In the basement are mechanical and electrical equipment, storage, and a loading/receiving area. On the first floor, the circulation/reference desk remains in the original building, while the addition includes a long reading room and a presentation room. The second level is dominated by the expanded reading room combining old and new spaces, with study tables that occupy more than half of the total floor area, predominantly along the perimeter glass walls. The addition also includes powerful new computer systems and software, significant new book-display shelves, group study areas, reading tables, a staff meeting room, and a copy room. In the original reading room, one sees the floating roof's support system: treelike concrete columns and starlike concrete spacers that elevate the roofs above the tops of the walls, creating a gap all around that maintains the floating illusion.

TOP: *Biomedical Library*
BOTTOM: *Cellular & Molecular Medicine East*

Outside, the addition is covered with panels of glass and aluminum, in contrast with the old building's recast concrete panels. However, since the new building picks up the proportions of the original, the combined complex comes together as a pleasing whole.

Alexander's original library is a testament to the talents and imagination of an architect who once worked in the office of famed Los Angeles modernist Richard Neutra. In mathematical terms, Alexander's roof is a series of hyperbolic parabolas, curved forms that result from the manipulation of straight lines. The addition included a significant technology update, including Wi-Fi throughout the building and the digitization of many materials formerly only available in books.

6. Palade Laboratories for Cellular & Molecular Medicine
Moore Ruble Yudell with Ratcliff Architects, 1991

Cellular & Molecular Medicine East
Moore Ruble Yudell with Lee Burkhardt Liu Architects, 1995

Fantasy is a word often used to describe the architecture of the late Charles Moore. These buildings along Library Walk, just south of Gilman Drive, combining classical and modern forms with a dash of Disney, came late in Moore's career and sum up the wild combination of rational thinking and out-of-this-world fantasy that was his signature. The buildings consist of parallel wings connected on the north end and configured in a long U shape around a terraced courtyard.

Medical school facilities in these buildings include the Glycobiology Core Facility (carbohydrate structural and monosaccharide analysis), the Histology/Hybridoma Core Facility (histological, immunohistochemical, technical, and interpretive services), and the Vector Development Lab (gene therapy research).

Gilman Drive curves around the northwest side of the complex. From this approach, the Palade building appears with long expanses of greenish glass on two levels, defined by horizontal floor slabs that project to form balconies and with columns and railings lining the edges of the balconies. In addition to the two above-ground levels, the building has a partially subterranean level with low clerestory windows that admit natural light; bulky equipment is out of view in sunken storage bays.

Balconies also run the length of the north side of this complex, which connects the two wings. The corners of the north end, along Gilman Drive, are anchored by concrete-block towers of concrete. On the east side, along Library Walk, Moore's complex takes on a richer, more urban appearance. A four-story pinkish conference tower midway along this side of the building is visible from a distance. Mature trees

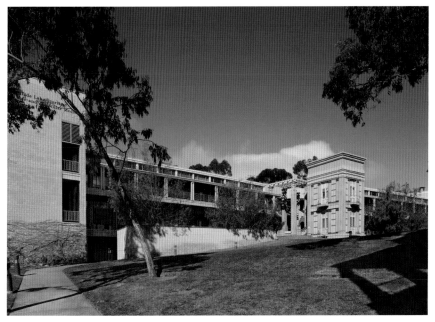

George Palade Laboratories for Cellular & Molecular Medicine

soften the edges of the building. Behind a low concrete wall is a small garden to be enjoyed by the building's occupants.

The south end of the complex is open to the landscaped courtyard at the heart of the medical school. From the medical school's grassy plaza to the south, a lawn slopes up into the space between the two parallel wings. At the top of the slope is artist Jackie Ferrara's *Terrace*, a public art piece in the form of a terraced courtyard that ties these buildings together. Broad steps on each side of *Terrace* lead to compact courtyards tucked in the corners of the mirror-image L-shaped wings.

In the crook of the west wing is one of UCSD's most mysterious and imaginative spaces. A semicircular stone bench creates a cloistered seating area beneath a two-story trellis supported by square columns. Behind the bench, through a small arch in a wall of concrete block and smooth granite, a circular fountain is tucked away like a hidden treasure. From the eaves above the top-floor balcony, godlike men of concrete, with bearded, angular faces, gaze down on the cloistered seating area.

Moore's second wing frames the east side of the courtyard. In form and materials the newer structure mirrors the original building.

Moore left an important legacy in San Diego. His other buildings include the Church of the Nativity (1993) in Fairbanks Ranch north of San Diego; the Oceanside Civic Center (1988); and the California Center for the Arts (1993) in Escondido. His buildings combine functional concerns with surprising combinations of classical, modern, and whimsical elements. Moore's late-career prime came during the postmodern era of the eighties. While many other buildings of that era now look kitschy and dated, Moore's wildly imaginative designs, including these buildings at UCSD, are proving to be as timeless as tales by Lewis Carroll or J. R. R. Tolkien.

7. Terrace
Jackie Ferrara, 1991

Fascinated with the architecture of Charles Moore, artist Jackie Ferrara agreed to collaborate with the design team (including landscape architects Spurlock Poirier) to create artistic terraces connecting the two Cellular and Molecular Medicine buildings. Ferrara's landscape is part of the campus's Stuart Collection of public art.

Ferrara's work, which often features plazas, courtyards, and structures, is uniquely architectural. At UCSD, *Terrace* consists of two levels, one next to each wing of Moore's Cellular & Molecular Medicine building. The terraces are covered with gray gravel and planted with Australian willow trees. Walkways of patterned gray, green, red, and black slate tiles run through the centers of the terraces. Concrete benches line low walls that define the edges of the terraces.

Using simple materials and quiet forms, Ferrara creates contemplative spaces where scientists go for a shot of solitude and imagination. In the early nineties, she was among a new generation of artists whose work was integrated with architecture, landscapes, and public spaces. This approach began to offer a welcome

The Terrace

alternative to the "plop art" phenomenon of the eighties, when public spaces across the country were overrun with large steel sculptures that seemed like generic after-thoughts.

8. Center for Molecular Genetics
Leonard Veitzer, 1984

UCSD was so pleased with architect Leonard Veitzer's Center for Magnetic Recording Research at Warren College that the university's Facilities Design & Construction division invited him to replicate that building for the Center for Molecular Genetics. The newer building's plan, structure, and mechanical details are duplicates of the original, with only slight alterations.

The Center for Molecular Genetics includes the Digital Imaging and Microinjection Facility, as well as microscopy and image analysis in conjunction with the San Diego Supercomputer Center.

Like other UCSD buildings of its generation, the Center for Molecular Genetics is a spare, minimal design without decorative, nonessential detailing. This calm, quiet design makes a perfect foil for architect Charles Moore's adjacent Cellular & Molecular Medicine buildings, with their colorful materials, fantastical forms, and courtyard checkerboards of multihued tiles. As with many other modern buildings of its era, the Center for Molecular Genetics has a minimal landscape that serves to showcase the building, not compete with it.

The building rests at the western edge of the medical school's central grassy plaza. It consists of a low horizontal wing fronting the plaza, with a three-story wing behind it. From the plaza looking at its west side, the building looks low and modest. But around the corner to the south, the long main entry sidewalk runs in front of three stories of horizontal window banks set beneath concrete eaves. Mature trees rise to the second and third levels from beds planted with hardy shrubs and flowering plants.

On the south end, pocket gardens are hidden behind low concrete block walls, and on terraces created by the stepped back levels of the three-level section. Many of the gardens and terraces include container plants and deck chairs, giving the building's south end the appearance of a residential complex.

Strong connections between landscape and structure are a natural outgrowth of Veitzer's significant experience with residential designs, including single-family houses and student apartments at UCSD. Here, his modest scientific building brings subtle beauty to scientists and visitors engaged in rigorous work that has life-or-death implications.

TOP: *Center for Molecular Genetics*
BOTTOM: *W. M. Keck Building*

9. W. M. Keck Building

RBB Architects, 2002

Situated at the south end of the UCSD School of Medicine campus, the W. M. Keck Building incorporates low concrete-and-glass cubes and right-angle outrigger-like buttresses that reach into the landscape like the outriggers of many postwar modernist buildings in southern California. The thick concrete walls shield sensitive scanning procedures from outside interference. The desert landscape of drought-tolerant shrubs and spiky cacti is an ideal complement to the concrete architecture.

Known to medical students as the Functional Magnetic Resonance Center, the Keck Building contains anatomical and functional magnetic resonance imaging (MRI) for animal and human subjects. MRIs are internal snapshots of the brain taken slice by slice. Functional MRI works by measuring changes in blood flow during neural activity. It produces a moment-by-moment three-dimensional movie of the energy pathway inside the brain. For instance, these images can pinpoint the place in the brain that prompts finger-tapping or responds to Mozart.

The center contains four MRI machines. It was created by UCSD and the Salk Institute of Biological Studies to examine how the brain controls visual perception and attention, cognition, emotional responses, learning and memory, language development, movement, various levels of consciousness, and a range of brain disorders including schizophrenia and Alzheimer's disease. Projects involve collaboration among researchers specializing in psychiatry, psychology, neuroscience, cognitive science, and radiology.

Schizophrenia is a primary focus of research in the Keck Building. Using the latest scanning equipment, researchers explore regions of the brain that may cause hallucinations, disorganized speech, and erratic behavior. In one type of study, subjects perform tasks while lying inside the MRI machines as scientists explore how brain responses of schizophrenics compare with those of healthy individuals. They hope to discover new drugs to target these specific areas of the brain. UCSD researchers share digital images of the brain with their peers at UC Irvine—fast Internet connections and new imaging systems have made this practical. Once information is standardized and shared, researchers across the country can explore the variation in brain function during certain tasks. In one study, each institution used MRIs to examine the brains of people afflicted with chronic schizophrenia.

10. Pharmaceutical Sciences Building
CO Architects, 2007

New treatments developed from research at UCSD and other leading institutions are rapidly changing the face of medicine. The current generation of pharmacists is trained to practice in a complex world of new medicines, treatments, and cutting-edge technologies that require them to understand the interactions of complicated modes of treatment as well as all potential effects on the patient. Pharmacists are increasingly involved with managing patient care on an ongoing basis.

The Skaggs School of Pharmacy and Pharmaceutical Sciences opened in 2002. Thanks to a $30 million gift in 2004 from the Skaggs Institute for Research, this building was designed and constructed, allowing the school to consolidate operations that had previously been located in various campus buildings. The school was renamed the Skaggs School of Pharmacy and Pharmaceutical Sciences.

The school's four-story headquarters contains classrooms, a clinical pharmacy, treatment rooms, and laboratories for research in bioinformatics, pharmaceutical chemistry, biological sciences, and high-intensity computational studies.

Located at the south end of the medical school campus, the building accommodates as many as 300 students, plus an array of fellows and residents. Pharmacy students take many of the same basic science courses as medical students, which means that they are thoroughly prepared to work closely with physicians. Each floor houses complementary disciplines, with the hope that faculty, graduate students, and researchers from various specialty areas will share their knowledge with each other and collaborate. The pharmacy school also collaborates with other departments on campus, ranging from the San Diego Supercomputer Center to the Center for Marine Biomedicine at Scripps Institution of Oceanography, which looks to the ocean for sources of new drugs.

The new Skaggs School enhances UCSD's reputation as one of the nation's leading medical schools, one that takes full advantage of the university's position on the cutting edge of research and technology.

Pharmaceutical Sciences Building

WALK TEN: EAST CAMPUS ACADEMIC
AND HEALTH SERVICES

1. Campus Services Complex

Anshen + Allen, 1991/1992/2002

Situated west of Interstate 5, the Campus Services Complex is not a part of the East Campus proper, but it is a convenient place to visit along Voigt Drive before it crosses the freeway onto East Campus. The complex stretches behind a curved concrete-block wall that screens the buildings from Voigt Drive. The wall is pierced with small openings, and set behind a drought-tolerant landscape that gives the front of the building the look of a spiritual retreat somewhere in Arizona or New Mexico.

Service departments have offices here and, more importantly, they have spacious service yards, loading docks, and parking lots. The building's occupants include Facilities Management, Environmental Health and Safety, the campus Police Department, Fleet Services (university vehicles, many of them electric, hybrid, or natural gas-powered), Mail Services (which handles everything from large UCSD direct-mail campaigns to parcel shipping and receiving), and the main campus print-and-copy shop (which produces business cards, brochures, and bound documents). All of these together serve a campus population the size of a small town.

Behind the front wall, the complex extends with individual concrete block buildings that each house a different service. On the east side are the loading docks and a parking lot for cars, trucks, and other service vehicles. The loading docks feature sets of roll-up doors that open to service and storage bays. The docks are shaded by translucent awnings and feature tall clerestory windows that bring natural light to storage areas. Shade trees soften this expanse of asphalt and concrete block.

Along the west side, the desertlike landscape of cacti and other water-sipping plants continues along the edges of buildings, sidewalks, and entry walkways. While the building's back walls are plain concrete or concrete block, the front walls are yellow concrete block and tan stucco, which gives visitors a friendly impression. Yellow fabric awnings along the front of the building pick up the color scheme, provide shade above office windows, and bring a more intimate scale to the long walls. Although the complex's various occupants attract a steady stream of vans, trucks, and buses, the circulation plan directs utility vehicles away from the offices on the other side of the building. Even though it is a service center, the building still presents an inviting public face.

2. The Preuss School

HMC Architects, 2001

Grooming eight hundred underprivileged students for higher education, UCSD's Preuss School consists of an administration complex, an auditorium, a library with eighteen thousand books, five classroom wings, and a landscape that includes a

TOP: *Campus Services Complex*
BOTTOM: *The Preuss School*

central amphitheater for large outdoor gatherings. Buildings surround a courtyard, with the amphitheater as a focal point.

Students in the sixth through ninth grades at San Diego public schools are admitted to The Preuss School by lottery. When they graduate, the vast majority of students gain admission to top colleges and universities where they prosper in a variety of majors. They are often the first in their families to attend college.

The Preuss School, named in recognition of the Preuss family and made possible by the Preuss Family Foundation's $5 million gift, opened in 2001 in temporary space at Thurgood Marshall College on the main UCSD campus. The Preuss School is located at the intersection of Voigt and Campus Point Drives, near UCSD's East Campus of medical buildings such as Thornton Hospital and the Shiley Eye Center. The school benefits from its proximity to campus. Students from Preuss visit the UCSD campus for lectures, special events, walking tours, and picnic lunches.

Five two-story classroom wings fan out at the courtyard's east edge, with twenty-eight classrooms and four science labs. The wings are connected by covered walkways and trellises. The classrooms are wired for extensive computer use. Curved roofs shade clerestory windows that bring natural light to classrooms and labs. Garden courtyards between the buildings provide a mix of year-round greenery, seasonal color, and shade trees. The school includes large recreational fields for soccer, lacrosse, and other sports, as well as basketball and volleyball courts.

The Preuss School's curriculum for sixth- through twelfth-graders balances the arts and sciences. The maximum class size is twenty to twenty-five students. All students take four years of math, laboratory sciences, and English; three years of a foreign language and fine arts; and two years of history. The academic year and daily schedule are longer than what is typical at local public schools.

Young scholars come to The Preuss School from neighborhoods all around San Diego. When they arrive at the unfamiliar school they are total strangers, but the low, eye-catching buildings and gardenlike setting create a soothing atmosphere where students prosper.

3. Shiley Eye Center
Anshen + Allen, 1991

Shiley Eye Center's spirited design and elegant materials create a friendly environment for patients who seek state-of-the-art diagnosis and treatment for diseases of the eye ranging from glaucoma to cataracts and complex neural problems. The building brought together various functions of the Department of Ophthalmology: clinical work, research, education, and surgery. It contains research and treatment areas, office space, and indoor and outdoor areas for families and patients. An abundance of soft, even, natural light helps visitors feel at ease, and the wood paneled interior, polished stone floors, comfortable furniture, and garden views help create a friendly environment.

The building was the first to open on UCSD's East Campus, which also includes John M. and Sally B. Thornton Hospital and the Rebecca and John Moores UCSD Cancer Center. The Shiley Eye Center is a pedestrian-friendly building that makes many connections to the landscape. It sets a strong example for subsequent buildings. The site plan preserves natural canyons and open space. As the landscape matures, the campus looks more and more like a park that just happens to have

Shiley Eye Center

some buildings on it. Landscaping and pedestrian paths make the campus extremely user-friendly. The medical campus is one of the first developments in San Diego to use water-saving drip irrigation for such a large landscape—the East Campus covers forty-three acres.

The Eye Center consists of two long parallel wings—a two-story structure in front and a three-story structure behind it. An atrium connects the wings, and a vaulted metal roof gives the Shiley Eye Center a distinctive appearance.

In 2004, Anshen + Allen's $9 million renovation to the Shiley Eye Center added a library, conference room, research space, and space to support outreach efforts, including free vision screenings and glasses for children in underserved neighbor-hoods. The renovation was funded through gifts from Donald and Darlene Shiley and Arthur Brody.

Patients and visitors find comfort in a eucalyptus-shaded courtyard where tables shaded by umbrellas are surrounded by beds of cacti and succulents. In this quiet oasis, when the ocean breeze rustles through eucalyptus branches and their shad-ows dance on the concrete, everything is just right for a few moments.

The Eye Center's bold, simple forms and clear organization bring to mind San Diego's most famous concrete masterpiece: architect Louis Kahn's Salk Institute for Biological Studies, designed to meet the research requirements of polio-vaccine pioneer Jonas Salk. In fact, there is more than a passing connection between Salk and Shiley. Anshen + Allen architect Jack McAllister and David Rinehart both worked for Kahn in the sixties during the design of the Salk Institute. In 1995, Anshen + Allen designed a major addition to Kahn's masterpiece.

4. Hamilton Glaucoma Center and Jacobs Retina Center

Anshen + Allen, 2004

Since the Shiley Eye Center's opening, the East Campus has evolved as a center for new medical technology and a showcase for patient-friendly architecture. As the Shiley Eye Center's research expanded, Anshen + Allen returned to design a complementary research and clinical treatment center. The building contains both the Hamilton Glaucoma Center and the Jacobs Retina Center.

Glaucoma is the leading cause of blindness in the United States, and the glaucoma center contains labs and research facilities dedicated to finding innovative new ways to prevent and cure the disease. At the retina center, researchers hunt for solutions to retinal disorders such as macular degeneration, diabetic retinopathy, tumors, and hereditary disease.

A steel pedestrian bridge over the landscaped courtyard connects the Shiley Eye Center with the two-story building that houses the Hamilton Glaucoma Center and the Jacobs Retina Center. The steel-frame stucco building is designed to remain rock-steady in an earthquake, protecting sensitive equipment and safeguarding patients during surgeries. It contains clinical research spaces, wet bench and computer analysis labs, and offices.

From the East Campus's main parking lot, the building is hidden behind the Shiley Center and the Ratner Children's Eye Center. From the east, though, this building and the Rebecca and John Moores UCSD Cancer Center flank a wide, landscaped pedestrian mall, offering motorists approaching from the east a dramatic view.

Hamilton Glaucoma and Jan and Irwin Jacobs Retina Center

Drawing from their design of the Shiley Eye Center, the architects created a detached addition across from the original Shiley building. Landscape architects Andrew Spurlock and Martin Poirier of Spurlock Poirier designed the space between the original building and the addition. Their long courtyard garden, with its drought-tolerant landscape of tall grasses, shade trees, crushed stone, and small seating areas, provides a quiet escape for patients and their families, as well as a multisensory experience for those having vision problems. On warm afternoons, the landscape fills with floral scents and the sounds of rustling leaves and happy birds. Next to the courtyard, along the glaucoma and retina center's north facade, two wide horizontal bands of windows overlook the landscape.

The building's south side flanks the landscaped pedestrian mall between this building and the Rebecca and John Moores UCSD Cancer Center. This side is more flamboyant, with walls of greenish glass shaded by a trellis that slants up dramatically from the roof. Steel columns support the trellis and define a sheltered pedestrian walkway near the building next to landscaped areas and concrete benches.

5. Ratner Children's Eye Center
CO Architects, 1996

The treatment of children with eye problems is a specialized field. Patients, some of them too young to articulate what is wrong, need a friendly, comforting atmosphere, as half the challenge of providing them with medical care is helping them to relax during examinations. Physicians, for their part, require specialized equipment to diagnose and treat problems such as misaligned eyes.

The Anne F. and Abraham Ratner Children's Eye Center is part of the ophthalmology complex that also includes the Shiley Eye Center, the Hamilton Glaucoma Center, and the Jacobs Retina Center. Compared with the other buildings, the Children's Eye Center is smaller and more playful, like its patients. It welcomes visitors with triangular awnings that look like whimsical eye patches. Children and parents enter the building from the landscaped courtyard at the center of the eye-care complex. Near the entrance is a colorful tile mural.

In the reception area, a puffer fish floating in a large aquarium mesmerizes the waiting children. Daylight fills the space and a television displays animated movies. Dozens of toys, books, and board games provide endless ways for young visitors to forget why they are there in the first place. Exam rooms are painted red, yellow, green, and blue. Doctors wear casual clothes, including cartoon-character ties.

While the Ratners were being treated at the Shiley Eye Center, they met Dr. Stuart Brown, chairman of UCSD School of Medicine's Department of Ophthalmology. At that time, Brown told Mrs. Ratner that early treatment is the key to preventing chronic vision problems. Not only did the Ratners decide to

Anne F. and Abraham Ratner Children's Eye Center

finance the new Children's Eye Center, but they also endowed a chair for pediatric ophthalmology and they funded an "eyemobile" that travels around San Diego to provide exams, and, if necessary, glasses to children in underserved communities.

6. Thornton Hospital
SMP Architects, 1993

7. Ambulatory Care Center
SMP Architects and Delawie, Bretton, Wilkes Associates, 1993

Checking into the John M. and Sally B. Thornton Hospital is a little like visiting a luxury hotel in Palm Springs. Cars drop visitors in a landscaped circular porte cochere, where a valet in a bowtie would not look out of place. The entrance is a glass pavilion with slanted green metal roofs beneath a glass tower visible from the parking lot like a lighthouse in a fog. Just inside, a "concierge" sits at a dark wood desk at the end of a lobby with polished granite floors and Art Deco lamps. The lobby opens to a living-room atrium with groupings of contemporary furniture arranged on area rugs.

The 120-bed hospital is a general medical-surgical center for San Diego's most advanced medical, scientific, teaching, and research programs. With its residential scale and inviting design, Thornton Hospital marks a departure from typical hospitals of past decades. Most people who were unfortunate enough to pay a visit to a hospital in the sixties or seventies can remember plain white surfaces, shiny equipment, and lots of fluorescent lighting. Needless to say, those buildings were not very inviting. When hospitalization is necessary, the Thornton Hospital makes the experience much more pleasant.

High above the lobby, a line of narrow skylights filters soft natural light into the space. Balconies on the second and third levels feature Deco-style railings with curved sections. The "living room" and balconies all have views through a wall of glass to a landscaped courtyard with wrought-iron chairs around tables shaded by canvas umbrellas. Upper-level hospital rooms have bay windows that provide courtyard views. In the elevator hallway at the atrium's edge, contemporary console tables and framed mirrors flank the elevator doors. In their rooms, patients can order room service from a restaurant menu twenty-four hours a day. In addition to the friendly architecture, the landscape by Wimmer Yamada and Caughey transforms the sizeable parking lot into smaller parking areas bordered by lawns, low hedges, mature trees, and low-maintenance shrubs. (Joe Yamada worked on UCSD's first campus master plan.)

The Ambulatory Care Center, adjacent to the hospital, is designed with the same proportions and with the same tan stucco and green glass as the hospital. It contains three levels: two floors above grade plus a basement.

The center provides specialized outpatient services ranging from internal medicine to oncology and orthopaedics. It includes a pharmacy, several dozen examination rooms, labs, physical therapy spaces, a radiology area, and a cast room (for setting broken bones with plaster casts). Locating these outpatient services outside the main hospital makes them more easily accessible to patients. It also frees the hospital to focus on the more immediate needs of inpatients who require more intensive care.

Next to the Thornton, the four-story Sulpizio Family Cardiovascular Center opened in 2010. RTKL Architects' design mirrors the Thornton Hospital's extensive glass and jewel-like facets. The Cardiovascular Center unifies UCSD's patient care, clinical research, and training programs for patients under heart and stroke care. The building includes more than twenty examination rooms and four cardiac catheterization labs. The new building is designed to take advantage of views of the La Jolla coastline, canyons, and Torrey Pines State Reserve, a showcase for the rare, gnarly pine species. In the spirit of its gorgeous natural setting, the Cardiovascular Center also includes an outdoor entry atrium, water features, healing gardens, and a courtyard.

John M. and Sally B. Thornton Hospital

The Edith & William M. Perlman Ambulatory Care Center

8. Moores UCSD Cancer Center
Zimmer Gunsul Frasca Partnership, 2005

Patients come seeking treatment, but first-time visitors to the Rebecca and John Moores UCSD Cancer Center must think they have arrived at some sort of entertainment venue. And that's a good thing! The building's front wall glistens with glass panels and green shingles of stainless steel. An aluminum-and-glass awning shades visitors from harsh daylight. In the three-story entry atrium, steel-and-glass staircases slant up toward the wood-paneled ceiling. Underfoot, the floor is a checkerboard of white, gray, and black linoleum.

The Cancer Center consolidates laboratory research, cancer prevention and control, clinical treatment, and administration—in the medical business, they call this all-in-one approach "bench-to-bedside." Cancer patients have access to essential outpatient services in one location. As many as 150 clinical trials take place simultaneously, evaluating medications aimed at everything from smoking cessation to breast cancer prevention, gene therapy, and pain management.

The architects' goal was to house the major research and treatment operation in a large building with an intimate, residential appeal. Like the Thornton Hospital, it even has a sizable, comfy "living room." The center consists of two structures: a three-story clinical services and administrative/educational building, and a five-story research center. The structures are connected to the atrium lobby and surrounded by gardens (designed by landscaped architect Katherine Spitz) that offer intimate, private seating areas. In the first-floor bamboo garden, for instance, teak patio furniture is arranged in groupings that seat six to eight people, and the greenery is dense enough that the building interior itself is barely noticeable. The second-floor patio features umbrella-shaded tables set in a container garden.

Rebecca and John Moores UCSD Cancer Center

Zimmer Gunsul Frasca's design utilizes forms of various shapes and sizes to make this large building seem like a friendly village. Because of the many balconies, decks, pedestrian bridges, and different landscapes, patients are transported to a colorful and interesting environment that can take their attention away from the deadly disease they are battling.

Waiting areas outside cancer treatment rooms have comfortable furniture and warm colors, encouraging patients to imagine they are in a living room instead of a medical office. They also feature rich wood detailing, and large glass windows and doors that look out on the gardens. Flooring ranges from pale green carpeting to checkerboard vinyl floor tiles.

Bridges connect upper levels, giving patients the sense that they are away in their own intimate world. Even the hallways are friendly, with their wood paneling, patterned ceilings, soft wall-mounted lights, and intimate groupings of designer furniture. And what other cancer center do you know that hosts an annual luau and surfing contest to raise awareness and funds for cancer treatment? You'd be impressed to see physicians, scientists, and business executives trade their lab coats and sport coats for board shorts and surfboards, paddle out past the breakers, and cut some crazy lines through the excellent waves near Scripps Pier in La Jolla.

La Jolla Institute for Allergy & Immunology

9. La Jolla Institute for Allergy & Immunology
Delawie Wilkes Rodrigues Barker, 2006

Colorful, inviting, and thoughtfully landscaped, the three-story La Jolla Allergy & Immunology building is the first in the thirty-acre UCSD Science Research Park that includes sites for several more buildings in the years ahead. This building demonstrates how far the architecture of science has come since San Diego's earliest research parks opened near UCSD during the sixties and seventies. The building's design sets a high standard for the many new buildings to be built around it in the new science park. If their architects follow this example, the park will be both a vital hub for research and a visual asset to the surrounding community.

Horizontal forms mirror the horizontal strata of nearby sedimentary rock from an ancient era when the ocean still covered this area. One reaches the building by car, but up close, the design of the Institute enhances the pedestrian experience. The low, colorful landscape and earth-toned hardscape take on bold geometric forms inspired by the building's forms. The landscape creates many intimate seating and meeting areas. A three-level atrium joins the north and south entrances; third-floor balconies provide an easy escape with a view.

Since UCSD was founded in the sixties on the research reputation of Scripps Institution of Oceanography, the university has consistently partnered with the private sector as a means of speeding progress. With several Nobel Laureates on the faculty and an international reputation for innovative interdisciplinary research, UCSD attracts nearly $730 million annually in research funding. The Science Research Park marks the latest phase of this synergy. Competition for technology companies has intensified among cities and universities, and the Science Research Park is an asset in sustaining San Diego's status as a prime headquarters city.

10. Mesa Childcare Center
Charles and Elizabeth Lee, 1992

Addition
Rob Wellington Quigley Architects, 2005

Designed using the scale, forms, and materials of a single-family home, the one-story Mesa Childcare Center makes day-to-day life easier for graduate-student parents who live in the adjacent Mesa Apartments. Two long buildings each have their own play yards shaded by deep eaves, mature trees, and fiberglass and canvas awnings. A rugged frame of steel I-beams supports the building and allows for an open and flexible interior.

Each building is divided into classrooms for children of various ages. Large windows and clerestory windows bring natural light to the classrooms. The building has a gently slanting gabled roof, exterior walls of horizontal wood siding, and pale green trim that matches the leaves of surrounding eucalyptus trees.

Quigley's 2005 addition offers a modernist contrast to the original building. Its minimal, cubic forms are rendered in wood siding, stucco, concrete block, and glass—maintaining some of the original building's character. Offices and classrooms look out on a play yard shaded by mature trees. The site's landscape of trees, lawns, and small shrubs surrounds both the original building and the addition, creating a parklike, child-friendly complex.

Mesa Childcare Center

ACKNOWLEDGMENTS

UCSD Campus Architect and Associate Vice Chancellor Facilities Design and Construction Boone Hellmann provided guidance and sage advice. Professor Alain Cohen and UCSD Associate Vice Chancellor for Campus Planning Jeff Steindorf supplied important background information Michele Humphrey, Dolores Davies, and Julie Dunn from the university's Communications and Publications departments gave essential feedback. Daniel Aruta in Facilities Design & Construction poured over the plans and provided fascinating details about the engineering of Scripps Pier. Jamie Intervalo and Chuck Kaminski in Boone's office kept the project organized. Architectural photographers David Hewitt and Anne Garrison made us proud of UCSD's architecture. Project editor Linda Lee at Princeton Architectural Press made countless constructive suggestions. Much gratitude goes to the architects from the past and present who inspire us with their imaginative designs. Special thanks to Mary Beebe, founding director of the Stuart Collection, for curating one of the finest collections of public art on the planet. H. P., Henry, Joann, Adam Sr., Sally, Berta, Hannah, Semira, Ben, and Bill are my concrete foundation.

INTRODUCTION

1. Esther McCoy and Randell L. Makinson, *Five California Architects*, 2nd ed. (Los Angeles: Hennessey & Ingalls, 1975).

2. Judith and Neil Morgan, *Roger: A Biography of Roger Revelle* (La Jolla, CA: Scripps Institution of Oceanography, 1996).

3. Patricia Aguilar, *The UCSD Master Plan and its Antecedents* (La Jolla: The Regents of the University of California, 1995). Aguilar's report is an overview of planning at UCSD up until that time. It is available in the Geisel Library at UCSD.

4. Ibid.

5. Robert Mosher, interview with the author, spring 2009.

6. Ibid.

7. A. Quincy Jones, *A Master Plan for University Center* (La Jolla: The Regents of the University of California, 1966).

8. Aguilar, *The UCSD Master Plan and its Antecedents*.

9. Boone Hellmann, interview with the author, spring 2009.

10. The faculty and administrative leaders who were involved in creating the new Master Plan and succeeding district (or neighborhood) studies which kept this plan vital included Nada Borsa (Associate Director – Physical Planning), Stanley Chodorow (Professor and Associate Vice Chancellor – Academic Affairs), Alain Cohen (Professor), Tom Collins (Associate Vice Chancellor – Marine Sciences), Patricia Aguilar (Director – Physical Planning), Ruth Covell (Associate Vice Chancellor – Health Sciences), John Goodkind (Professor), Ted Groves (Professor), Newton Harrison (Professor), Walter Heller, Jr. (Professor), Campus Architect Boone Hellmann, John Holland (Professor), Wayne Kennedy (Vice Chancellor – Administration), David Miller (Professor and Associate Vice Chancellor – Academic Affairs), Walter Munk (Professor), A.W. Russ (Associate Vice Chancellor – Undergraduate Affairs), Frieder Seible (Professor), George Shor (Professor), Fred Spiess (Professor), Jeffrey Steindorf (Associate Vice Chancellor–Campus Planning), Debra Wingard (Professor), and John Woods (Vice Chancellor – Resource Management and Planning).

11. Aguilar, *The UCSD Master Plan and its Antecedents*.

12. Ibid.

13. Artists in the Stuart Collection: Terry Allen, *Trees* (1986); Michael Asher, *Untitled* (1991); John Baldessari, READ/WRITE/THINK/DREAM (2001); Jackie Ferrara, *Terrace* (1991); Ian Hamilton Finlay, UNDA (1987); Richard Fleischner, *La Jolla Project* (1984); Tim Hawkinson, *Bear* (2005); Jenny Holzer, *Green Table* (1992); Robert Irwin, *Two Running Violet V Forms* (1983); Barbara Kruger, *Another* (2008); Elizabeth Murray, *Red Shoe* (1996); Bruce Nauman, *Vices and Virtues* (1988); Nam June Paik, *Something Pacific* (1986); Niki de Saint Phalle, *Sun God* (1983); Alexis Smith, *Snake Path* (1992); Kiki Smith, *Standing* (1998); William Wegman, *La Jolla Vista View* (1988).

14. Stuart Collection, http://stuartcollection.ucsd.edu/StuartCollection/index.htm, University of California, San Diego.

15. UCSD Campus Community Planning Committee, *Long Range Development Plan* (La Jolla: The Regents of the University of California, 2004).

WALK ONE

1. Skidmore, Owings & Merrill, *UC San Diego 1989 Master Plan Study* (La Jolla: The Regents of the University of California, 1989).

2. UCSD Campus Community Planning Committee, *UC San Diego 2004 Long Range Development Plan*.

3. Ibid.

4. Patricia Aguilar, *The UCSD Master Plan and its Antecedents* (La Jolla: The Regents of the University of California, 1995). Aguilar's report is an overview of planning at UCSD up until that time. It is available in the Geisel Library at UCSD.

5. Ibid.

6. The Birch Aquarium, http://aquarium.ucsd.edu/, University of California, San Diego.

7. Sam Hinton, *The T. Wayland Vaughan Aquarium-Museum* (La Jolla, CA: Scripps Institution of Oceanography, 1958).

8. Deborah Day, *William Aaron Nierenberg Biography* (La Jolla, CA: Scripps Institution of Oceanography, 1997).

9. William Turnbull, "Scripps Hillside Neighborhood Planning Study," University of California, San Diego, http://physicalplanning.ucsd.edu/PPW-PlansStudiesProjects/N-Studies/siohill.html.

10. Deborah Day, "History of the Old Director's House," California Sea Grant, http://www-csgc.ucsd.edu/ABOUTUS/RitterHistory.html.

11. Hinton, *The T. Wayland Vaughan Aquarium-Museum*.

12. Deborah Day, *Harald Ulrik Sverdrup Biography* (La Jolla, CA: Scripps Institution of Oceanography, 2002).

13. Research on Scripps Pier's structural details provided by Daniel Aruta, UCSD Facilities Design & Construction.

WALK TWO

1. Antoine Predock, "Body/Motion," Antoine Predock Architect, http://www.predock.com/Body-Motion/machines.html.

WALK FOUR

1. George Mandler, interview with the author, spring 2009.

2. Modern San Diego, "Richard George Wheeler: 1917–1990," http://www.modernsandiego.com/Wheeler.html. "Architecture Views," written by Richard George Wheeler, was found among the architect's papers following his death in 1990.

WALK FIVE

1. Jorge Mariscal, *Brown-Eyed Children of the Sun: Lessons from the Chicano Movement*, 1965–1975 (Albuquerque: University of New Mexico Press, 2005). Mariscal is a longtime professor at Warren College.

2. Ibid.

WALK EIGHT

1. Alain Cohen, in interview with the author, summer 2009.

All photographs © Anne Garrison and David Hewitt unless otherwise noted.

Pages 13, 23 UC San Diego, Glasheen Collection/Mandeville Special Collections Library

Pages 14, 16, 22 bottom, 24, 25 UC San Diego Libraries, Scripps Institution of Oceanography Archives

Page 18 Marine Corps Recruit Depot San Diego

Page 22 top Robert Alexander

Page 30 Skidmore, Owings & Merrill

Page 32 UC San Diego Stuart Collection

INDEX